CRAFT 4.0

New perspectives of making

Edited by

Giuseppe Lotti
Marco Marseglia
Elisa Matteucci
Giulia Pistoresi
Eleonora D'Ascenzi

DESIGN EXPERIENCES

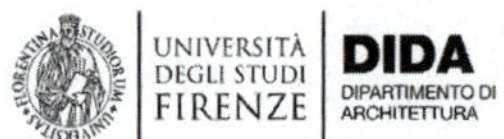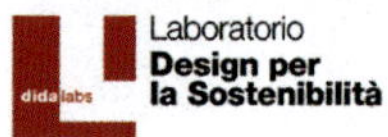

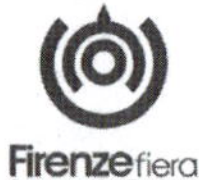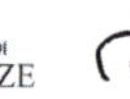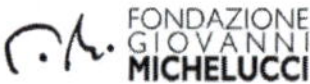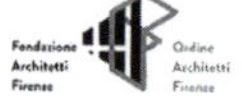

Craft 4.0 was born on the occasion of MIDA |
Florence International Crafts Fair 2021 as a reflection
on one of the many declinations of contemporary
craftsmanship - new perspectives of making.
The introductory texts make *Craft 4.0* not only
a catalog but also a book that questions the
relationship among craftsmanship, innovation,
technology, and design with a specific focus on social
and environmental implications.

CONTENTS

PREFACE

THE NEW PERSPECTIVES OF MAKING: CRAFT 4.0

Lorenzo Becattini
President of the Firenze Fiera Administrative Council

Craft 4.0 is part of *New perspectives of making*, a series of exhibitions dedicated to new scenarios of artisanal innovation, promoted by the *Florence International Crafts Fair* - MIDA. All this also aims at a stimulating and in-depth reflection on the different phenomenology of 'craftsmanship' started with the exhibition *Dov'è l'artigiano* curated by Enzo Mari in 1981.
The first exhibition of the series, *Circular Craft*, took place at Fortezza da Basso in 2019 and was dedicated to the contribution of craftsmanship to the challenge of circular economy. The exhibition, curated by the Department of Architecture - DIDA of the University of Florence with the participation of Legambiente Toscana, presented detailed examples of craft businesses acting on the reuse-recycle of waste and scrap materials from industry or separate collection.
In *Craft 4.0*, presented in the 2021 online edition of MIDA, the scenarios presented are those of technological craftsmanship in view of the strategies of enterprise 4.0. The event was curated, along with DIDA, by the Municipality of Florence, the Foundation of Florence Architects, and the Giovanni Michelucci Foundation. The pandemic restrictions led us to create a virtual exhibition, inevitably losing the 'visual' and 'tactile' charm of admiring the works live, but with the awareness of a present-future where the two exhibition forms - real and virtual - will increasingly coexist.
The main objective of the exhibition, in which internationally renowned designer craftsmen from all around the world - from France to China - participated, was to show the products and processes of the new craftsmanship with specific attention to technological innovation, without losing the value of heritage and manual skills, and with particular attention to design processes and experimentation also on a conceptual level.
The experience of *Craft 4.0*, together with the many ones promoted in recent years within the International Crafts Fair, makes MIDA a fundamental point of reference for craft companies and systems on a national and international level.

FLORENCE BETWEEN TRADITION AND INNOVATION

Carlo Francini

Site manager of the UNESCO World Heritage site "The Historic Center of Florence"
for the Municipality of Florence

Florence is often defined with high-sounding and grandiloquent epithets: one of the most famous is certainly that of "cradle of the Renaissance".
In itself, this definition reflects a fundamental characteristic of the history of our city, but it is likely to become a sign of immobility and tiring repetition, so much that it is often spontaneous to think of a cradle where to fall asleep and live blissfully, anchored to ancient glories.
Florence has been, above all, a creative city that has known how to renew itself over the centuries, with greater or lesser audacity, without betraying its past.
The cultural heritage, both tangible and intangible, that characterizes Florence and that has allowed the entry of its historic center in the World Heritage List in 1982, finds its identity in the continuous elaboration of thoughts and actions.
Nothing could have been realized in those extraordinary works surrounding us, if there had not been this constant collaboration between masters, students and intellectuals.
Today we are called to continue in this direction, ready, as always, to innovate - looking for the best and most appropriate technology that can allow us to create new things - and not to be satisfied with what we have achieved.
In this way, we will not betray our heritage but, on the contrary, we will keep it alive, ready to pass it on to future generations.
We should always examine and learn more about our past as a source of inspiration to be open, inclusive and vibrant.
Bringing up to date the experience of Medieval and Renaissance workshops - an osmotic exchange of different and complementary skills - should be, with a continuous tension balancing between tradition and innovation, the aspiration of the new artisan workshop.
Post-pandemic Florence should be able to take up this challenge, creating the conditions for this to happen in a natural continuity with its extraordinary tangible and intangible cultural heritage.

VANISHING POINT 4.0

Jean Blanchaert

Gallerist, art curator and art critic

We do not want to question the Archbishop Marcel Lefebvre's purity of heart, but his strenuous opposition to the Second Vatican Council, announced by Pope Roncalli in 1962 and concluded by Pope Montini in 1965, was akin to a man stubbornly standing, with open arms, in front of a flooding river that is coming down, trying to block it. The river in question is time evolution. However, since it is a good thing, it is better to navigate this wave, trying to understand it and going along with it because no dam, no artificial barrier can stop the flow of history. Back in 1968, a year before the actual moon landing on July 16th, 1969, the artificially intelligent supercomputer HAL 9000 on the spaceship Discovery, in Stanley Kubrik's film *2001: A Space Odyssey*, spoke to the ship's commander David Bowman. It sounded like science fiction, except that a few months later, Neil Armstrong and Buzz Aldrin were hopping and driving an "off-road vehicle" over the Sea of Tranquility, and the Earth, seen from so far away, seemed to Neil Armstrong "smaller than a golf ball". In any case, it was a breathtaking vision, not the Stendhal syndrome. As soon as he set foot on lunar soil, Armstrong named and honored Galileo Galilei, the true father of modern physics, who four hundred years earlier had formulated the theory of gravitational acceleration with a purely mental experiment. In connection with 600 million people, Armstrong dropped a hammer and an eagle feather that touched the Moon at the same time, confirming Galileo's theory.

This extraordinary event is placed at the beginning of the digital age, the Third Industrial Revolution in the Western world. The first one was in 1784 with the birth of the steam engine, the second one was in 1870 with the advent of the internal combustion engine. Today, in 2022, we are in the midst of the Fourth Revolution that is leading to automated and interconnected industrial production. The term Industry 4.0 was first used at the Hannover Fair in 2011 in Germany. In 2012, a working group dedicated to Industry 4.0 presented a set of recommendations for implementation to the German federal government, and the following year, the working group's final report was released at the annual Hannover Fair. Claude Lévi-Strauss said that the craftsman is "the prince of innovators" and this characteristic is present even when, in recent times, he/she makes use of the support of new technologies. It is he/she who decides how far to go and where to stop in order not to dehumanize the artifact.

NEW PERSPECTIVES OF MAKING | CRAFT 4.0

The marble works we see today are usually made by two types of craftsmen: the contemporary one, the engineer who guides the robot rough-hewing the work of art; the ancient, classical one who completes it, refining it. In addition, it is important to remember that from Hellenism onwards sculptors had the possibility of using the drill, the "gimlet", which allowed them to pierce the marble reaching otherwise unreachable points. Let's take three examples: Laocoön, Giovanni Pisano, and Gianlorenzo Bernini. As an innovation, it is equivalent to today's computer.
New technologies can be mixed with traditional craftsmanship with a combination of manual and digital skills. A robot (a word derived from the ancient Slavic *rabota* meaning heavy work) is any machine capable of doing more or less independently the work of a man, succeeding in some cases in making numerous products that, with the right devices, become unique pieces.
This is not always possible. The 1200 degrees reached during the processing of blown artistic glass allow only manual interventions by the glass masters.
This exhibition is so refined that the curators have thought to divide it into five categories: (*Craft.4.0*) for human, (*Craft.4.0*) for work, (*Craft.4.0*) for nature, (*Craft.4.0*) for community, (*Craft.4.0*) for culture. We can admire works that, although they are created with new technologies, are beautiful and have not lost their soul.

CRAFT 4.0, AN EXHIBITION

Giuseppe Lotti

Dean of Bachelor's Degree in Industrial Design, University of Florence

The *Craft 4.0* exhibition has been organized for MIDA 2021 and Firenze Fiera by the Department of Architecture of the University of Florence, the Municipality of Florence, the Foundation of Florence Architects and the Giovanni Michelucci Foundation.
The exhibition has been edited by Marco Marseglia, Alessandra Rinaldi, Elisa Matteucci, Eleonora D'Ascenzi, Giulia Pistoresi, Manfredi Sottani, Marika Costa, and me, but generally speaking by the Sustainable Design Laboratory of the Department of Architecture.
Craft 4.0 shows us a part of the future craftsmanship, namely the artisan skill of being contaminated by technological innovation.
Enterprise 4.0 is an actual scenario characterized by:
1. hyper-connection
2. intelligence
3. automation
and, therefore, it represents a smart scenario.
We often think that Enterprise 4.0 technologies are mainly available for big companies and highly technological sectors. Traditionally, Enterprise 4.0 scenarios are presented starting from enabling technologies:
- internet of things
- mixed reality (augmented and virtual reality)
- value-added manufacturing
- cloud
- big data...
but it's difficult to understand the real effects of these solutions on our lives. Certain of the importance of technology and at the same time attentive to it: "... on what can you rely instead? Technology? That's an even riskier gamble. Technology can help you a lot, but if technology gains too much power over your life, you might become a hostage to its agenda (...). Technology isn't bad. If you know what you want in life, technology can help you get it. But if you don't know what you want in life, it will be all too easy for technology to shape your aims for you and take control of your life (...). Of course, you might be perfectly happy ceding all authority to the algorithms and trusting them to decide things for you and for the rest of the world. If so, just relax and enjoy the ride. You don't need to do anything about it. The algorithms will take care of everything. If, however, you want to retain some control of your personal existence and of the future of life, you have to run faster than the algorithms, faster than Amazon and the government, and get to know yourself before

they do. To run fast, don't take much luggage with you. Leave all your illusions behind. They are very heavy" (Harari, 2018-2020, pp. 349-351).
This is all we need to introduce an Italian way of using technological innovation in the Made in Italy field. Technologies without any doubt, but with a meaning… With environmental, socio-cultural and economic sustainability as ultimate goal: *"Una riflessione sulla nuova rivoluzione industriale sarebbe priva di senso se non venisse inquadrata nelle prospettive globali proposte dalle Nazioni Unite, come essenziali per lo sviluppo dei prossimi decenni. Intendere Industria 4.0 solo come la messa in linea di robot per la produzione di beni commerciali, o ridurre 4.0 alla digitalizzazione delle attività di produzione e scambio individuali, senza tener conto della dimensione dei problemi che oggi si aprono al mondo globalizzato, sarebbe svilire il senso stesso di 'rivoluzione' che si vuol dare a questa trasformazione produttiva. L'emergere di necessità di intervento su queste aree tipicamente definibili come beni pubblici dimostra come si aprano opportunità di sviluppo per economie capaci di coniugare capacità di innovazione produttiva e apparati scientifici e tecnologici in grado di affrontare grandi sfide globali, la cui mancata soluzione minaccia di costituire devastanti esternalità negative per la crescita dell'intero pianeta (...) Se Industria 4.0 si limitasse alla risoluzione dei problemi legati al consumo individuale, non avrebbe quel carattere di sconvolgimento generale che un'espressione così impegnativa come rivoluzione industriale implica; il banco di prova più significativo per la 'produzione digitale iperconnessa' sarà affrontare il grande tema dei beni comuni, cioè come gestire in tempo reale i grandi temi della vita collettiva di oggi, dal cambiamento climatico alla gestione dei grandi centri urbani, dalla sicurezza di tutti al diritto di ognuno alla privacy"* (Bianchi, 2018, pp. 68-70).
The *Craft 4.0* scenarios are divided into 5 sections:
(*Craft 4.0*) for human
(*Craft 4.0*) for work
(*Craft 4.0*) for culture
(*Craft 4.0*) for community
Each section exhibits 2 products.
We have chosen experimental products, in-between design and art - almost manifest products - able to tell us something about the possible future:
- the mix between 3D printing and manual processing
- crossing technologies and nature
- circular economy challenges

- the role of algorithms for creating products
- the importance of the platform in order to involve the communities…
But *Craft 4.0* also points out present and future events. It is a virtual exhibition. From a technical point of view, the exhibition presents:
- complete freedom of use
- the potential of the "virtual" vehicle in terms of space management
- different levels of insights - increased information
- the companies can use the exhibition as a promotional tool
- possibility of reaching many people
- reduction of the environmental impact (we are working to quantify it).
We believe in the importance of real exhibitions (we need relationships, empathy, coffee… and they also give employment to many people…), but the future will undoubtedly be characterized by the coexistence of these two forms of expressions.

References

· Bianchi P., 2018, *4.0 La nuova rivoluzione industriale*, il Mulino, Bologna.

· Harari Y. N., 2018-2020, *21 Lessons for the 21st Century*, la Repubblica, Milan.

THE CREATIVE CRAFTSMANSHIP BEYOND THE PRESENT MOMENT

Antonio Bugatti

Foundation of Florence Architects

Dealing directly with the realization of an idea, without any interpositions, is the dream of all architects. The connection between drawing and craftsmanship can now retrace old paths towards new perspectives in the fascinating track of artistic crafts.

When the production - together with new technologies and new models of representing design objects - directly involves craftsmanship, it embodies the ability to give substance to an idea-shape: thus, the product of the perfect synthesis between the graphic processing of an object and its material and usability is obtained.

Furthermore, if between the virtualization-design and the production of the object, the distances induced by the - sometimes too complex - testing phase are shortened, the quality and uniqueness of the result are definitely increased thanks to the creation of a high-value product, which makes both who made it and who will benefit from it proud.

This way of "proceeding", which goes back to the origin of craftsmanship since ancient times, has been brought back by MIDA in collaboration with the Foundation of Florence Architects. The latter is a cultural and promotional branch of the different types of professional employment supported by the Order of Architects with the aim of offering new opportunities to bring visibility to creativity, and to concretize ideas, within the perspective of drawing the proper attention of the MIDA wide audience in its next edition. While waiting for this, Craft 4.0 has explored and applied new virtual exhibition techniques resulting from the long phase of physical distancing due to the pandemic crisis.

All things considered, the major and persisting interests for architects are to overcome the mere implementation both from a creative design and from a manual point of view, and to visualize the "envisioned", even in these extreme conditions.

The connection between design and craftsmanship, recently brought back by the need to rediscover - in spite of everything - the original dimension, necessarily shows the role of the architect as the perfect interpreter and mediator between project and production with a predominantly artistic slant. This depends on what architects know about the new imaging techniques that connect their knowledge of shape and function with materials and construction techniques, in the perspective of a highly evolved artisan production compared to the consolidated tradition and to the way of interpreting the virtual representation of the object. In this way, many other themes are added, including immaterial design and the design application to the most visionary fields - even more suggestive in cognitive pathways - in the possibility of immediately approaching the idea of the object to its forthcoming, concrete and usable physicality.

MICHELUCCI AS A CRAFTSMAN

Andrea Aleardi
Giovanni Michelucci Foundation

Today, the debate about the confluence of the arts and the multidisciplinarity of different skills is revealing a new fertile ground for research and innovation exchange as well as experimentation in the design sector. Design should be considered in its remarkable "artisan dimension", maybe further from "Industrial design" in the narrow sense.
Our Foundation is dedicated to the grand master, Giovanni Michelucci, to his work as an architect and - above all - to his design thinking, looking at the City as "necessarily" variable in order to be always contemporary with its civil history. This interpretative key has recently developed interesting research sites following Michelucci's vision and a renewed relationship among Design, Craftsmanship and City.
In the past few years, not only in Tuscany, the interest for that perspective intended as "second architecture" has grown in these fields.
This approach has been strongly supported and valued by Giovanni Michelucci both on a critical and educational level since 1948 with the unforgettable issues of the magazine "Esperienza Artigiana", gathering architects, artists, artisans for a common ideal, and on a realization level in the collective experience started at that time at the Galleria Vigna Nuova in Florence and subsequently carried out for a long time on several design horizons.
He tells us in an editorial:
C'è chi pensa che una rivista che s'intitola "artigiana" debba occuparsi esclusivamente dei prodotti che si definiscono "artigiani" e non di opere di architettura, di scultura e di pittura [...] noi sappiamo che per ottenere un immediato particolare risultato "Esperienza Artigiana" dovrebbe diventare un ricco emporio di modelli da imitare e da copiare. Ma a noi preme qualcosa di più: preme cioè [...] che fra l'artigiano, l'artista e il pubblico si stabilisca quel rapporto di conoscenza e di cultura di cui si è parlato, presentando questa rivista.
[...] Quel senso di inseparabilità del cittadino attivo e della città [è] il significato civile che acquista il costruirsi la propria città: di lavorare, cioè, per produrre qualcosa di indispensabile, praticamente e spiritualmente, alla propria città; di operare per il benessere e la bellezza comune: per sé cioè e per gli altri cittadini (Michelucci, "Esperienza Artigiana", 1949).

This Michelucci's glance guides us and leads us to the present.
In a territorial context, as the Tuscan one, and in an educational and artistic context, not only the world of professional designers but also a large number of young makers, artists and "new artisans" are operating. They all address the issue of design and product: on one side with a new, strong, "native" technological operationality, and on the other with a particular sensitivity to traditions, history, materials and the storytelling of the process as an added value of the product itself, thanks to the production of the piece of art that should be, if not unique, undoubtedly personalized or even better enhanced for its uniqueness not only in its aesthetic but also in its realization value.
Nowadays, this raises the question of renovating the way to "make" design and/or applied art through new tools, collective work and an ethical dimension, for example in sustainability, for a contemporary vision of production that is rather close to the Michelucci's approach, meant to be a process model.
Creativity, sharing, experimentation, transmission of knowledge and experiences are the keys to face new challenges starting from the work of the Grand masters.

CRAFT 4.0: COMPLEX INTERACTIONS

Marco Marseglia

University of Florence

The *Craft 4.0* exhibition has been a contribution to the multiple possibilities offered by recent digital technologies that in the recent decades have allowed the world of design, and beyond, to embark on new paths of innovation and transformation. The new production techniques with more or less complex calculation and manufacturing systems hybridize with other techniques, leading to different ways of collaboration that we could define as Superintelligence (Bostrom, 2018). In the new paradigm offered by the 4.0 scenario, heterogeneous forms of human, mechanical, computational, collective and animal intelligence contaminate each other, increasing the complexity of the methods of making objects. Every system, as we all know, necessarily has to be increased in complexity in order to expand the number of relationships and interrelationships between its constituent parts (Gandolfi, 2008).

From the projects displayed in the exhibition, it is possible to understand that the context offered by new technologies addresses and transforms the creation and development processes of the artifacts by making human-technological hybrids, as in the project by Andrea Salvadori who uses ceramics with a mix of manual skills and 3D printing, up to hybrids combining technology with non-human elements such as bees and mushrooms as in the projects of Tomáš Gabzdil Libertíny and the Klarenbeek & Dros studio, where non-human elements become co-workers (Collet, 2017 in Lucibello, 2019). In the Studio Joachim-Morineau projects, the co-worker is instead the programmed printing system that regulates the rotation speed and the dripping flow of the ceramic material in order to generate ceramic structures open to imperfection and structural randomness.

Unlike industrial production, based on the non-coincidence of design and production, on the separation of work at an exponential level (Mari, 2004), in the scenario proposed by *Craft 4.0* the act of planning corresponds again with the one of creating the object by expanding, sometimes thanks to the digital, the interaction between the final product and people, as in Tim Knapen's "L'Artisan Électronique". The craft object becomes therefore an 'open work' leaving plenty of room for people who can model the object through a simple hand movement which, by changing the direction of a laser and an optical device, digitally models a vase, which is then 3D printed with ceramic.

"

In this case, 3D printing is not used as a pure programmed reproduction but as a co-creation where the subjectivity of the individual interacting with the machine always generates different solutions.

In the projects of Ching-sui Yang and Kourosh Asgar-Irani, new production methods - 3D printing and generative design - are mixed with traditional knowledge. Ching Hui Yang uses the brass casting technique by pairing jewelry with 3D printing while Asgar-Irani designs rugs that take up the Persian tradition, using software to manipulate the patterns in response to the layout of the room where they will be placed. The themes of customization and flexibility are two other elements that characterize this new production paradigm, offering the world of design and craftsmanship the possibility of combining skills, methods and operational approaches to respond to the request for product customization. Kniterate moves in this direction and creates a compact digital knitting machine that allows the manufacture of small quantities of customized fabrics.

In the case of Miko presented by Common Works, users are invited to design projects through an online virtual reality platform, using the movement of the smartphone, to model the object, subsequently handcrafted, with the aim of involving and entertaining people in the manufacturing process.

Studio Swine, instead, creates unique pieces by recovering plastic from the seas in a new idea of factory finishing the waste material of human beings to safeguard the planet and reveal that the world is characterized by imperfection. Precisely the imperfection and sometimes the randomness bring together the projects, presented in *Craft 4.0*, in a new model that uses digital technologies but with a view to a post-digital production model (Alexemberg, 2011) involving the human and the non-human.

References

- Alexemberg M., 2011, *The Future of art in a Postdigital Age*, Intellect Ltd, Bristol.

- Bostrom N., 2018, *Superintelligenza. Tendenze, pericoli, strategie*, translated by Simonetta Frediani, Bollati Boringhieri, Turin.

- Gandolfi A., 2008 (I Ed. 1999), *Formicai, Imperi, Cervelli. Introduzione alla scienza della complessità*, Bollati Boringhieri, Turin.

- Lucibello S., 2019, *Design, Natura e Artificio: verso un nuovo modello autopoietico?*, "diid, disegno industriale|industrial design", Design e Scienza n. 69/2019.

- Mari E., 2004, *La valigia senza manico. Arte, design e karaoke. Conversazione con Francesca Alfano Miglietti*, Bollati Boringhieri, Turin.

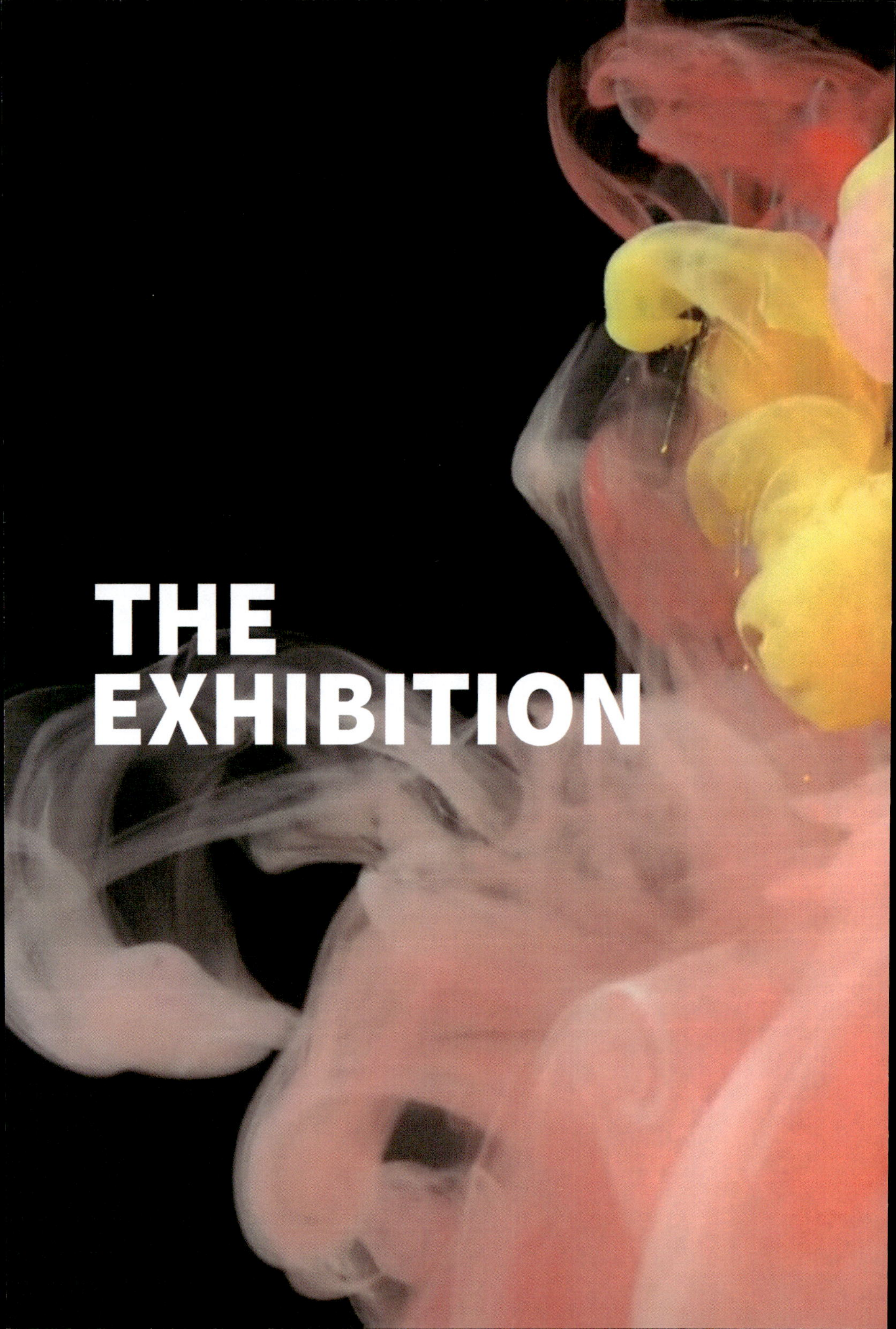

THE
EXHIBITION

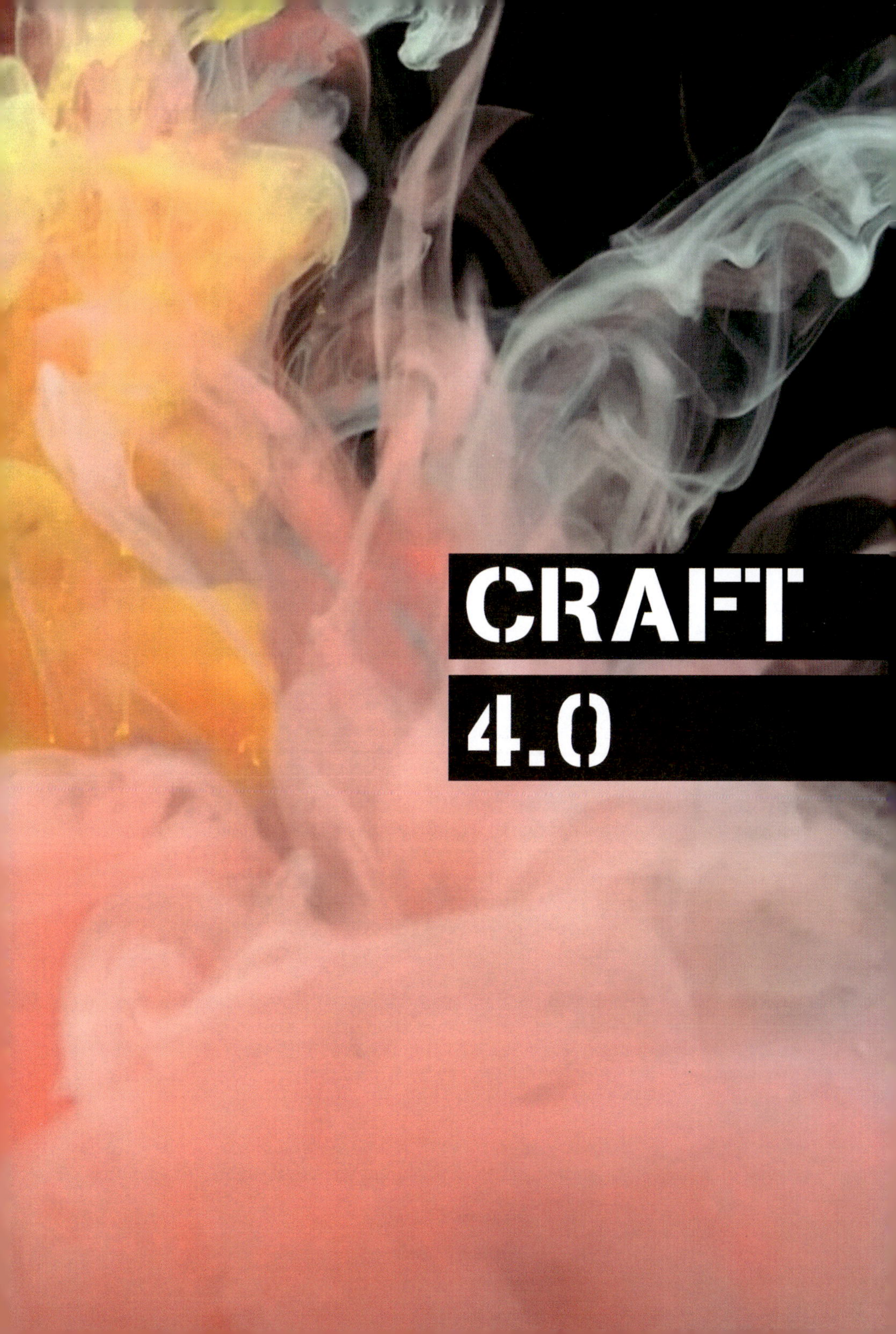
CRAFT
4.0

NEW LAYERS OF INTERACTIVITY
A possible dialogue between technology and craftsmanship

Elisa Matteucci
University of Florence

The art of making, creating and manufacturing, in its most traditional sense, is undergoing a major change due to the evolution of technologies and the development of more and more sophisticated "machine learning" devices. The ability of some devices to replicate or assist human gestures as well as the desire to guarantee uniqueness and quality, typical of manual work, to the object mechanically produced, offers the possibility to imagine new scenarios that respond more specifically to contemporary needs. In this respect, we could refer to this kind of hybridization between technology and craftsmanship with the expression Critical Making, coined by Matt Ratto. This concept defines:

"a mode of materially productive engagement that is intended to bridge the gap between creative physical and conceptual exploration. Although they share much in common with forms of design and art practice, the goal of these events is primarily focused on using material production - making things - as part of an explicit practice of concept elaboration within the social study of technology". (Ratto, 2011)

For the "purists", tied to an exclusively traditional approach of craftsmanship, this combination with 4.0 technologies may seem illogical, but this is undoubtedly a new form of collaboration: it does not impoverish or replace in any way the traditional approach to craftsmanship, but it rather integrates the latter by offering new ways of expression and new aesthetic and formal languages. In his works, Ingold often refers to artisan thinking that is powered by the synergy between body, productive gesture, material and work tools. It is evident that the concept does not change if we include technology among these factors.

This process of transduction is the meeting point between continuous and persistent paths that influence each other and that are able to generate new possible developments. Technology adds new possibilities to craftsmanship. This is true not only for technologically advanced devices or tools, but also for new materials or technologies that implement the characteristics of traditional materials.

In conclusion, it is reasonable to think that emerging technologies are not a way of delegitimizing traditional craftsmanship. New technologies and craftsmanship can coexist simultaneously in order to create "other" experimental solutions aimed at responding more precisely to the ecological, social, cultural and technological changes of the contemporary world.

References

· Ratto M., 2011, *Critical making: Conceptual and material studies in technology and social life*, "The information society", 27: 4, 252-260.

THE "DESIGN OF A VIRTUAL EXHIBITION"
The evolution of exhibition spaces and its related advantages

Giulia Pistoresi
University of Florence

Exhibitions have always been places where people are impressed, inspired, and pushed to learn. Therefore, such places enrich people from both cultural and emotional perspectives.

Over the years, exhibitions have adapted to the needs of an ever-changing society. Nowadays, they can be divided into two main domains which mark our daily life: physical exhibitions, and virtual exhibitions.

The MIDA 2021 exhibition has been virtually developed in response to the current COVID-19 pandemic, raising the issue of the coexistence between traditional knowledge and technological innovation.

Thanks to the great diffusion of the digital language in modern society, which has decreased the difference between tangible and intangible, the concept of experience has completely changed. Hence, virtual exhibitions have become a natural evolution of the traditional ones.

Virtual exhibitions completely redefine both the traditional design methodologies of an exhibition and the user experience.

The curatorship of a virtual exhibition opens up new scenarios and possibilities. Such results are clear from the design of MIDA 2021. Indeed, the selection phase of projects to be displayed did not have any difficulties related to transportation or logistics. The design of the exhibition spaces has been developed through an unconventional approach, adapting to the virtual format. Instead of traditional tools, such as plants and sections, MIDA 2021 shows storyboards capable of simulating the user experience, focusing on the user's perception.

Craft 4.0 scenarios have been classified into five categories, depending on the impact of technology application. The categories are nature, human, culture, work, and community. Each one of them is virtually located in a specific exhibition area, where a big screen shows emotional videos to emphasize the topic. Thanks to digitalization, which leads to dematerialization, the exhibition includes uncommon content. For example, there are floating objects, disproportional artifacts, the realization process of the displayed works, and different levels of interpretation.

As previously mentioned, also the user experience may vary. Users can freely move in the virtual space of the exhibition. There are no constraints in the itinerary, allowing the user's instinct to guide the exploration of the space. Users are encouraged to learn, but they can decide the level of insights they want to gain, the duration of the visit, and the order of the works. Moreover, the virtual format allows everybody around the world to access the exhibition without any geographical or temporal barrier.

In conclusion, even though the virtual format cannot guarantee the multisensory experience, typical of physical exhibitions, it is undeniable that the digitalization of exhibitions has contributed to the dissemination of culture and knowledge, especially in this delicate historical period. From this perspective, physical and virtual exhibitions should be considered as two distinct means, whose coexistence and integration could lead to greater involvement and distribution.

THE CRAFT 4.0 TALK:
The debate about the role of technology in craftsmanship with the leading designers

Eleonora D'Ascenzi

University of Florence

Due to the current pandemic emergency, the organization of exhibitions has been reconsidered not only in light of virtual experience but also through its integration with virtual talks. Exhibitions, whether virtual or real, are nowadays embracing the complexity of current problems and challenges through the displayed objects as well as through debates and talks, by integrating purely technical aspects with qualitative ones.

A clear description of the exhibited objects is sometimes provided directly through a talk conducted by the authors. This aspect becomes fundamental to understand the logic of curatorship and the explanation of the designers' vision. Furthermore, the interaction among designers is sometimes not just a dialogue between participants and speakers, but rather an interaction only between speakers.

This type of talk, alternated with questions and comments between peers, can be assimilated to a focus group where everyone is free to talk about their own project, leaving some time at the end for the group discussion. The MIDA 2021 talk is characterized by this kind of formula, allowing the public to directly interact with internationally renowned actors thanks to the abolition of geographical, temporal and linguistic limitations.

The designers invited to the talk come from many different countries (Austria, France, Belgium, etc.) even though they all live in Holland: this aspect undoubtedly reflects the innovative power of design that is present in that area. To ensure a wider dissemination, the MIDA 2021 talk was held in English and simultaneously translated into Italian in order to virtually show the displayed projects. This format allowed the public to intervene and to ask questions in real-time.

The talk started with the introduction of Giuseppe Lotti who highlighted the nature of craftsmanship and its recent contamination with technological innovation. He focuses on the new application of Industry 4.0, no longer restricted to big companies, that is fundamental today for those technological implications which could contribute to the competitiveness of artisan production. After that, Giuseppe Lotti explained the 5 sections of the exhibition, illustrating the importance of the crossing between technology and nature, technology and human, technology and work, technology and culture, technology and community. By doing so, he underlined the impact of experimental products and their possible innovative openings towards the future.

Afterwards, there was the screening of an emotional video that briefly summarizes the virtual exhibition with an overall vision and a focus on some manifest products. At the end of the presentation, designers showed their projects taking turns, and clarified their concept ideas and the relationship between technology and art. They even explained the encountered difficulties in implementation.

The designers described the objects and the related creation processes, allowing the audience to fully understand their ideas thanks to an overall view that moved from the very early concepts to the adopted methodologies.

Specifically, the talk hosted the following speakers: Tim Knapen with his "L'Artisan Électronique" in collaboration with Unfold, Studio Joachim-Morineau with "Moca", Studio Ching-Hui Yang with "Im-perfect", Kourosh Asgar Irani with "Rugture", Tomáš Libertíny with "Eternity aka Nefertiti".

The focus group model was encouraged by the questions the speakers made to their colleagues, intrigued by the projects exhibited, meanwhile and after participants intervened and asked questions in real time. This format allowed direct interaction not only between designers, but also between designers and audience. The talk has been intentionally reported as a live transcription to ensure a faithful report of designers' interview. The talk highlighted the concept of designers by explaining the works and the adopted processes. The idea of "thinking out of the box" together with the mixture of technology and art were the *fil rouge* of the event. Everything was seasoned with the common will to experiment, going beyond their own comfort zone, crossing the line of knowledge marked up to that moment.

Tim Knapen, together with Unfold, made a digital ceramic platform to create an intuitive and fun interface, making the pottery available for all people without any specific need for previous design knowledge. According to Tim Knapen, technology must be seen as a tool and not as the final aim, since, if it were considered "magical" and completely relied on this idea, a serious mistake would be made and the projects would lose their meaning.

Studio Joachim-Morineau, instead, showed how a serial production of unique ceramic pieces is possible thanks to the use of parametric technologies. In this case, the challenge is to combine technological uniqueness and imperfection.

Carla Joachim and Jordan Morineau underlined the importance of a continuous research approach, also demonstrated by their "Moca" project. This is still to be defined and subject to continuous improvements among all the difficulties, including learning new elements such as programming and coding errors. The approach strongly recommended for those who want to undertake a similar path is to "plunge headlong" and contaminate each other as much as possible: an approach that they have adopted and continue to adopt also from the comparison of their duality and different thinking.

Ching-Hui Yang, in her studio and through her master's thesis, has placed particular emphasis on the importance of design as a tool for emotional communication. In this case, the combination of technology and craftsmanship is given by the type of creation of the objects. Sometimes made through 3D printing, sometimes through the more traditional manual technique, sometimes as a mixture of both techniques, this project aims to tell the acceptance process of disabilities through the production of different works. The latter, with different forms and materials, represent the different emotional steps of acceptance. The difficulties encountered by Ching-Hui were initially related to the characterization of the individual objects and then, as indicated by herself, under the suggestion of her tutor, to the involvement of people in design through surveys and interviews.

Kourosh Asgar Irani, on the other hand, with his "Rugture" project, talked about the combination between craftsmanship and technology using the application of parametric design (started during university in the architecture sector) in the textile field. In this case, the result is given by technological innovation and the more traditional field of carpet design. In addition, the mixture of technology and craftsmanship has allowed the conjunction between the architect's Persian family tradition and his studies. Kourosh highlighted how the project encountered some difficulties within the chosen workshops but also how this made his project unique by emphasizing the importance of the birthplace.

Tomáš Libertíny concluded the talk by drawing attention to the peculiarity of his project which combines 3D printing (used as a base) and craftsmanship, thanks to the interaction with nature. His design object was in fact created through the collaboration of 6,000 bees who swarmed over a vase-shaped beeswax frame. Thus, his project is the concretization of the relationship between technology and nature, and its result is the perfect deal with cultural heritage. Progress, in this case, guarantees cultural dissemination.

On the whole, this talk has revealed the different approaches of the designers who try to face one of the most touching challenges of today: the combination of craftsmanship and technology without the supremacy of one component on the other.

NEW
PARADIGMS

The categories

Industry 4.0 represents a scenario characterized by hyperconnection, intelligence, automation. Therefore it is a smart scenario, in evolution, not yet fully defined and with different variations. Traditionally, Industry 4.0 is symbolized by enabling technologies - Internet of things, mixed reality (augmented and virtual), cloud, big data, etc. - but it is difficult to understand the tangible effects of these solutions even for professionals and, even more, for the general public. At the same time, the use of such technologies are considered to be available exclusively to large companies in high technological sectors but not for the traditional ones of our country.

The *Craft 4.0* exhibition makes visible the possible positive implications of 4.0 technologies in everyday life. A specific focus should be on artisan manufactures that through these solutions can contribute to the productions' competitiveness to attribute content and meanings to technological innovation.

All this to foreshadow an Italian way of technological innovation in the Made in Italy sectors. Technologies yes, but with meaning. The *Craft 4.0* scenarios are declined according to the application of technologies and they refer to 5 categories.

exhibition video

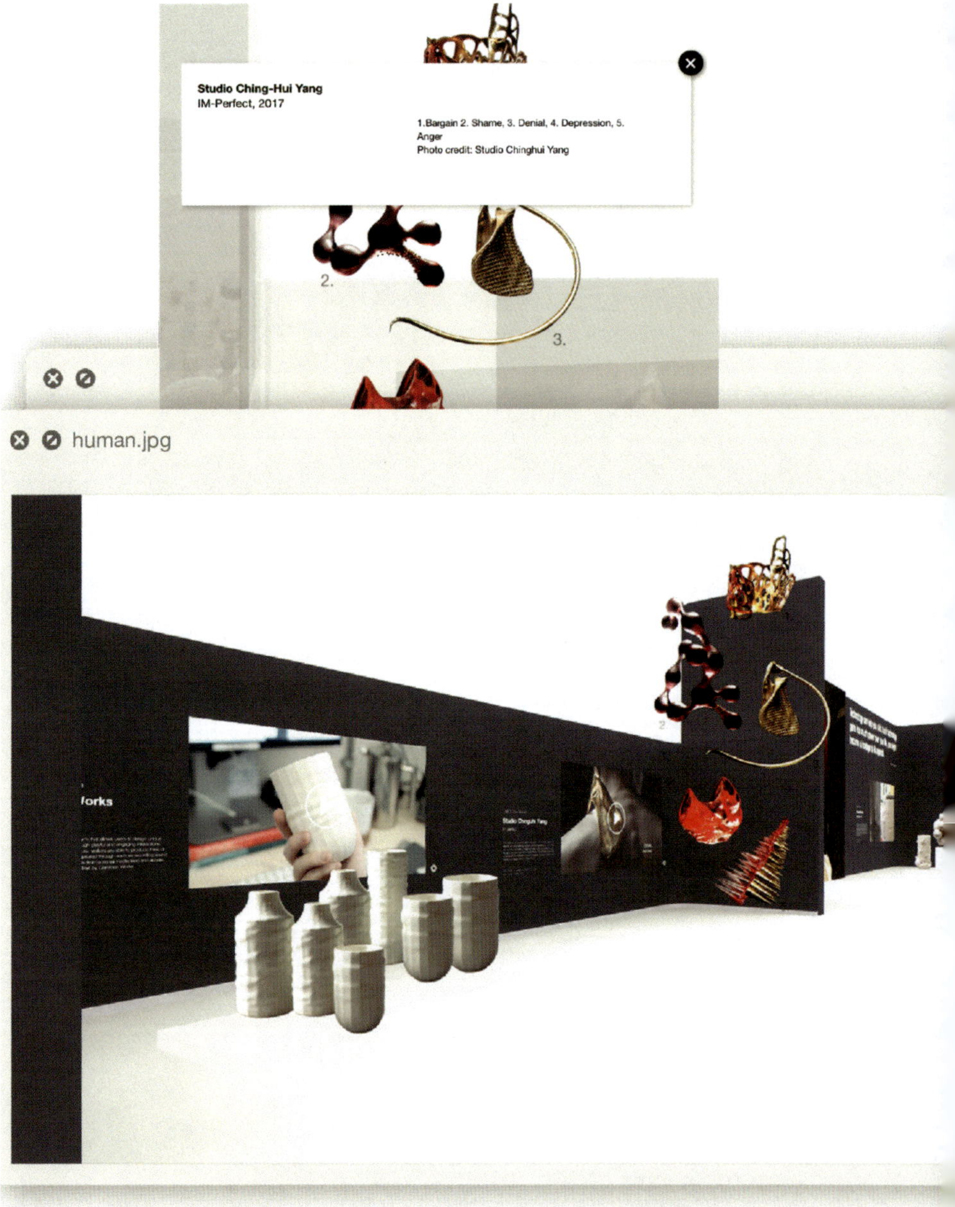

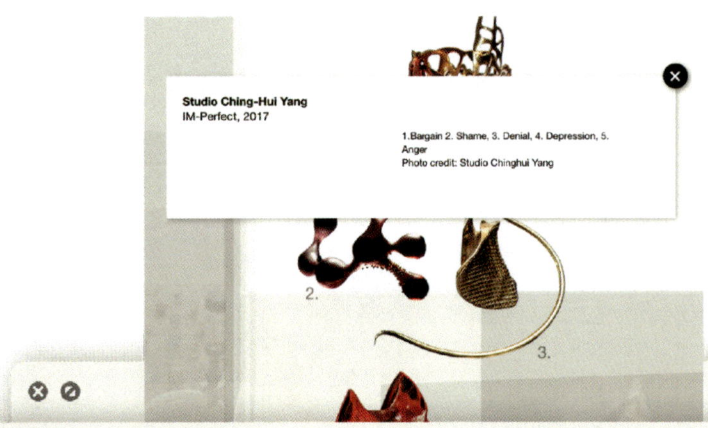

Studio Ching-Hui Yang
IM-Perfect, 2017

1.Bargain 2. Shame, 3. Denial, 4. Depression, 5.
Anger
Photo credit: Studio Chinghui Yang

human.jpg

CAN TECHNOLOGY CREATE SOCIAL INNOVATION?

(CRAFT 4.0) FOR HUMAN

Technology must be in the service of humanity. The Craft 4.0 revolution generates opportunities with a positive impact on people, starting from the most fragile categories, for an innovation that, to be considered as such, should be first and foremost social before being technological.

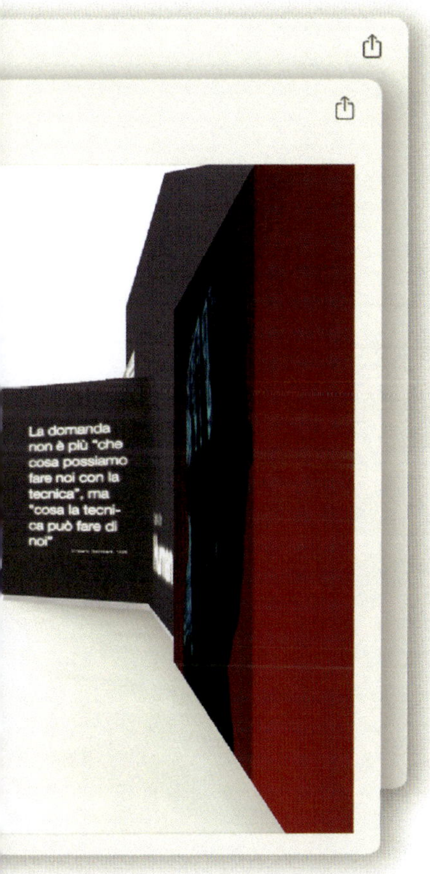

CAN TECHNOLOGY AID THE HUMAN WORK?

(CRAFT 4.0) FOR WORK

Technological innovation can hybridize with traditional craftsmanship on behalf of work. The use of new technologies should not be considered a threat but an opportunity to take advantage of new tools and thus raise the quality of the product through the combined use of manual and digital skills.

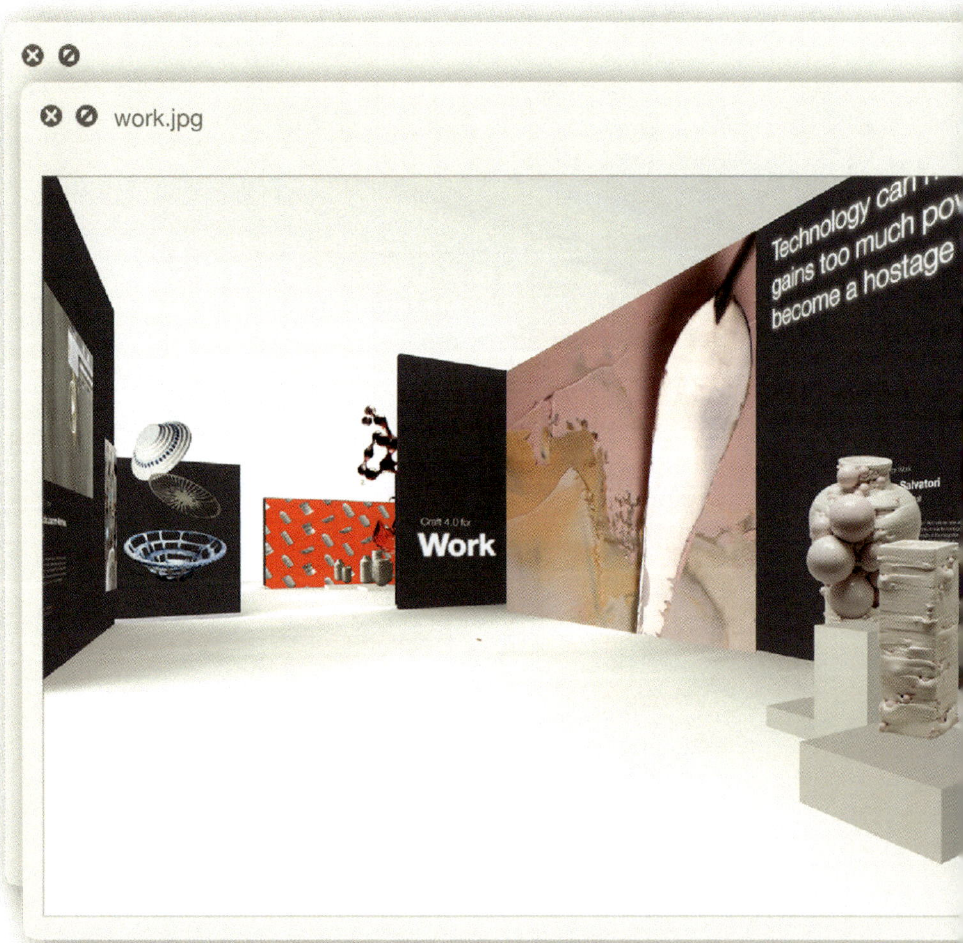

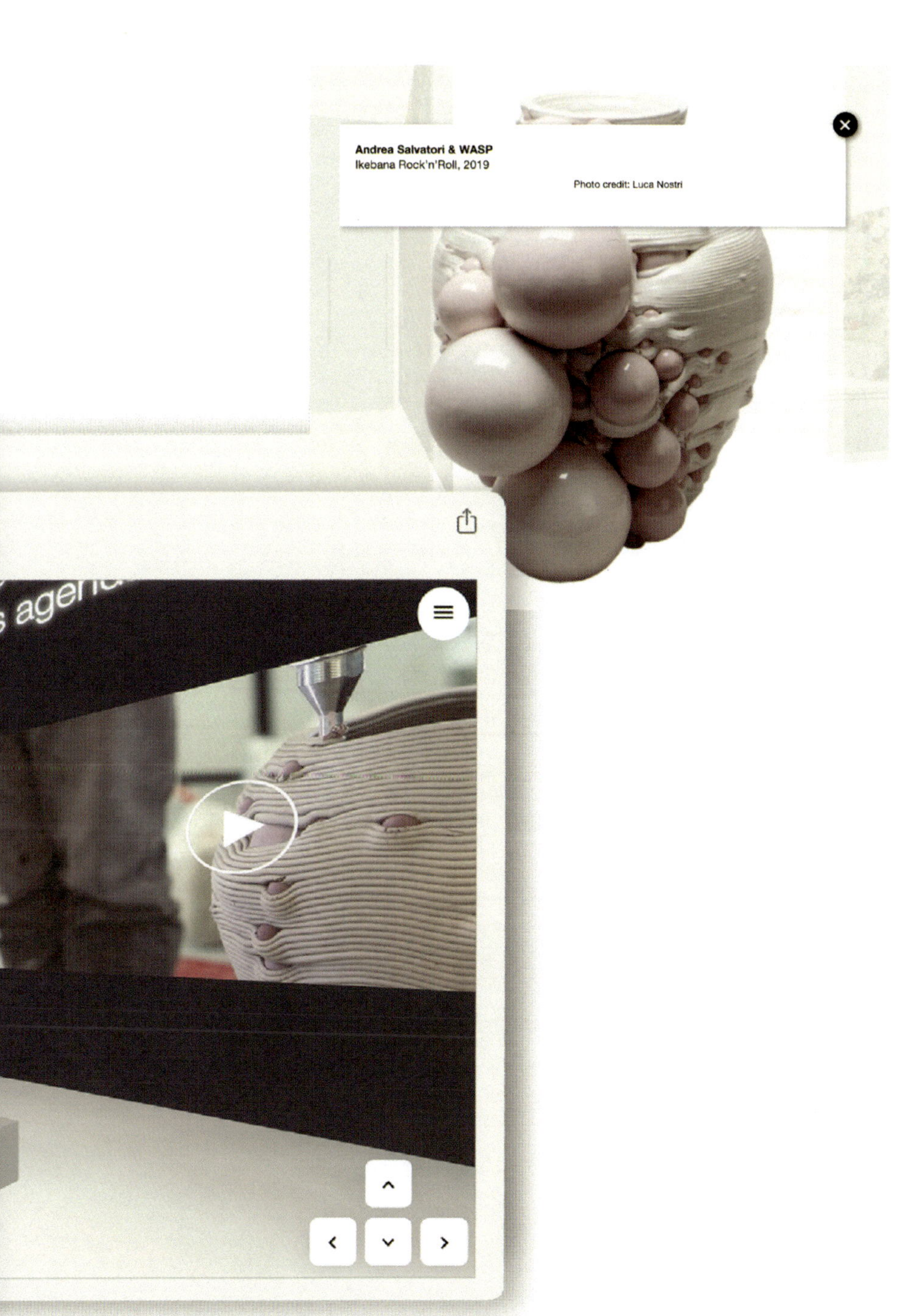

Andrea Salvatori & WASP
Ikebana Rock'n'Roll, 2019
Photo credit: Luca Nostri

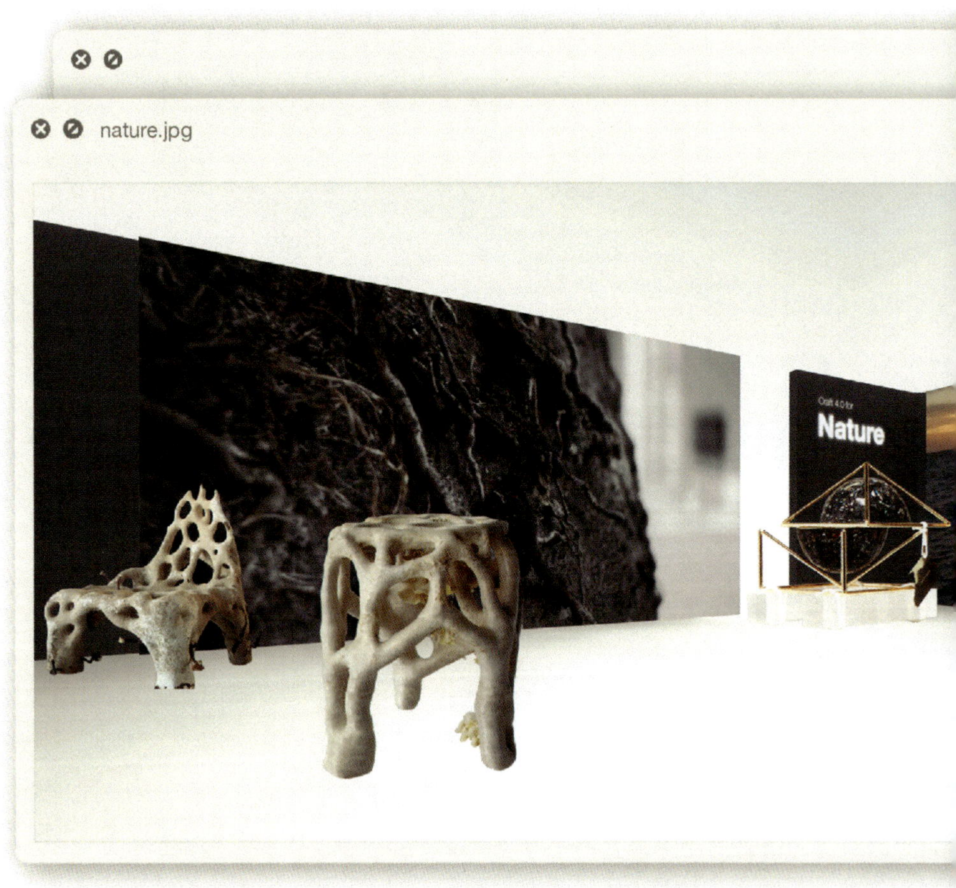
nature.jpg
Craft 4.0 for
Nature

CAN NATURE COEXIST WITH CRAFTSMANSHIP AND TECHNOLOGY?

(CRAFT 4.0) FOR NATURE

Can nature coexist with craftsmanship and technology? Especially in light of this pandemic scenario - with the virus that is the consequence of our wrong attitude towards the planet - we need to rethink the use of innovative technologies by highlighting the equal relationship between human and nature.

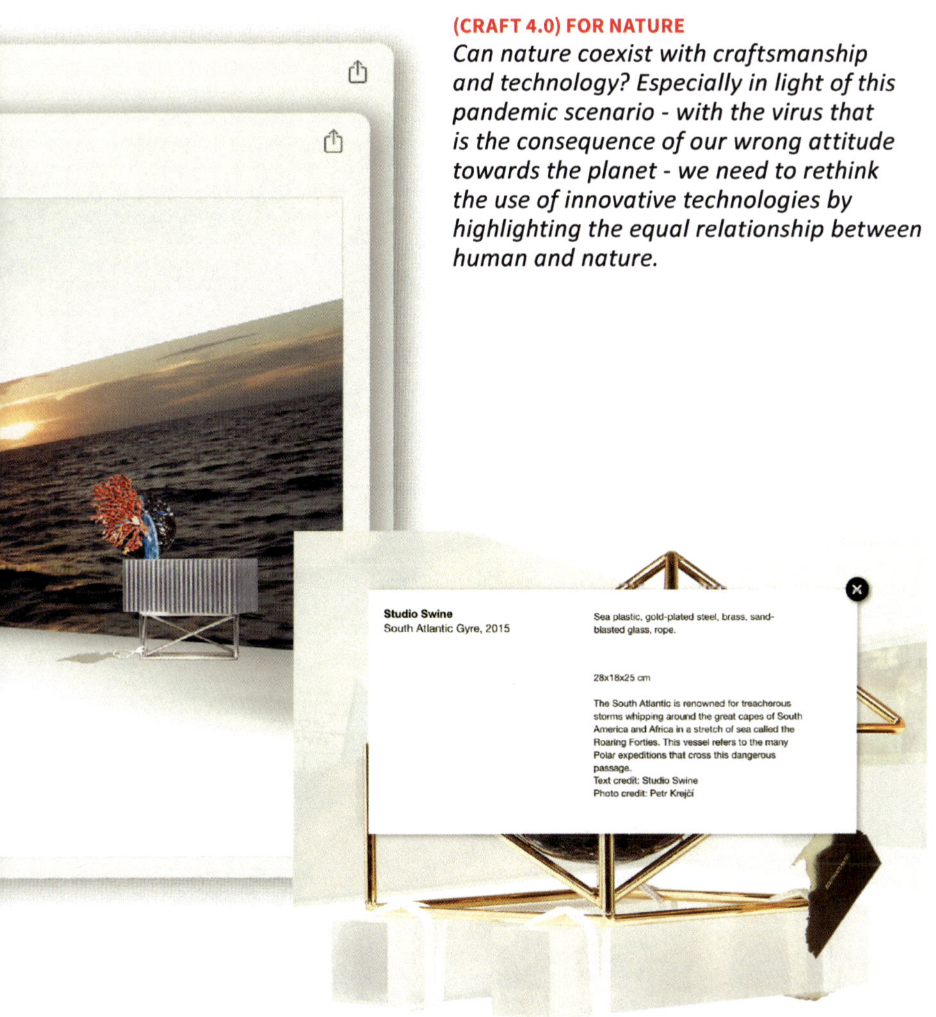

CAN TECHNOLOGY CREATE SENSE OF COMMUNITY?

(CRAFT 4.0) FOR COMMUNITY

The complexity of present and future social and environmental challenges requires the involvement of everyone. Technological innovation could help build more cohesive communities starting from a interests' sharing to promote effective policies and projects.

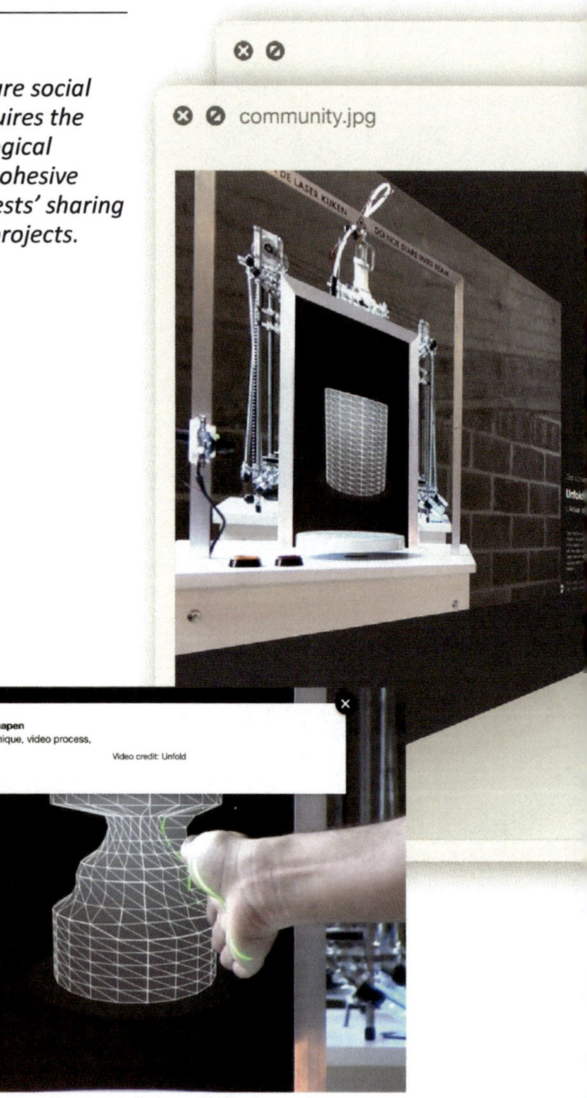

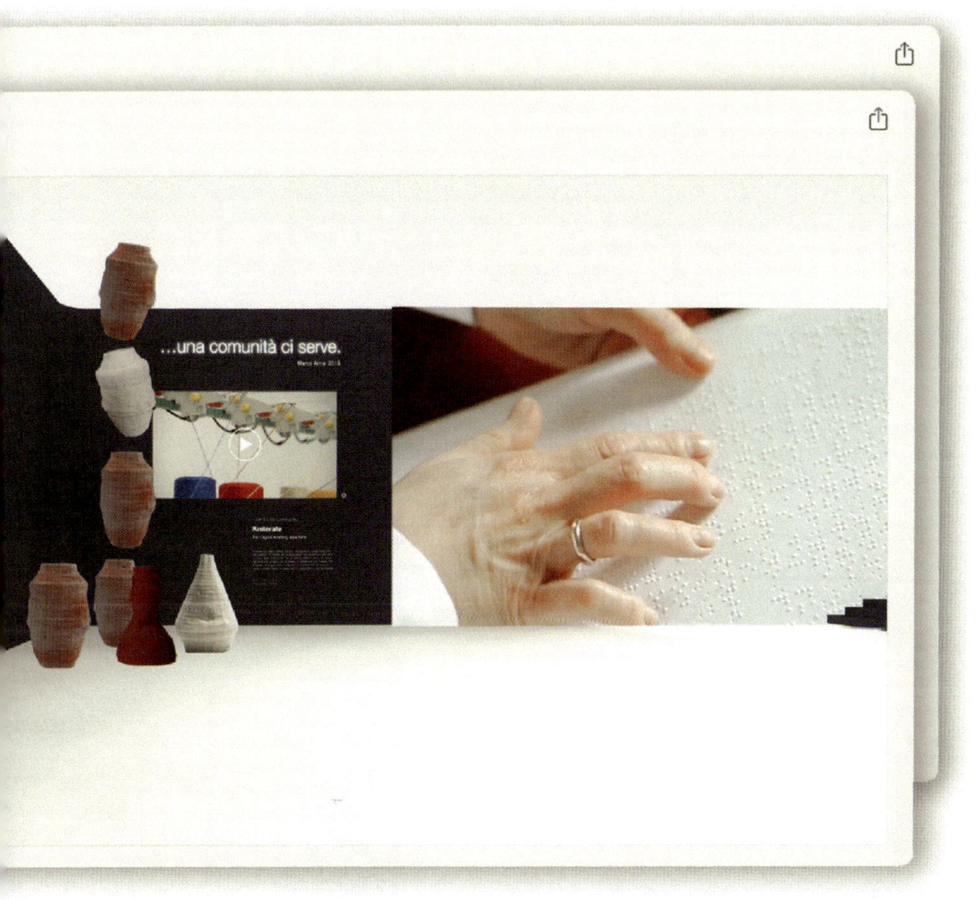

...una comunità ci serve.
Kniterate

CAN THE NEW TECHNOLOGIES ENHANCE THE CULTURE?

(CRAFT 4.0) FOR CULTURE

New technologies can actively contribute to the enhancement of cultural heritage. Guiding innovation towards the discovery and protection of cultural wealth represents one of the central contributions that technology can guarantee in favor of cultural heritage.
The sections of the exhibition are dedicated to each of the above-defined themes in order to build a frame of the multiple and various contributions.
The choice fell on highly experimental products within a scenario among craftsmanship, design and art with manifesto products able to show an already present future.

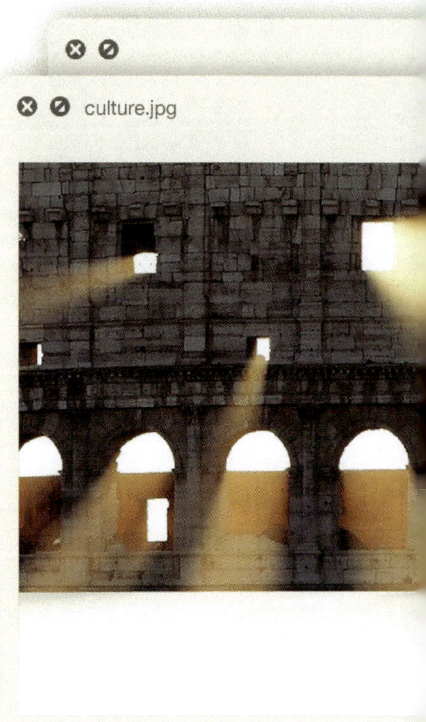

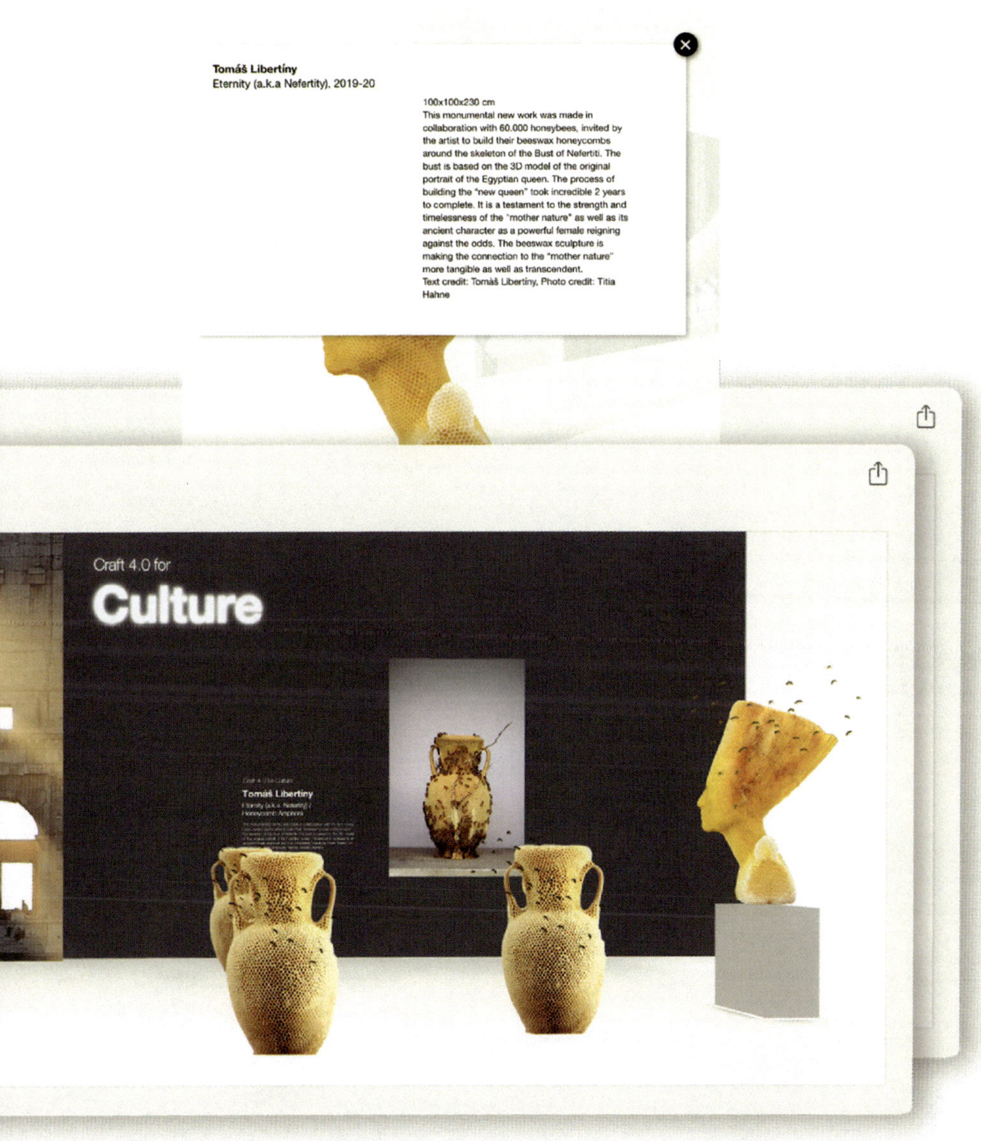

Tomáš Libertíny
Eternity (a.k.a Nefertity), 2019-20

100x100x230 cm
This monumental new work was made in collaboration with 60.000 honeybees, invited by the artist to build their beeswax honeycombs around the skeleton of the Bust of Nefertiti. The bust is based on the 3D model of the original portrait of the Egyptian queen. The process of building the "new queen" took incredible 2 years to complete. It is a testament to the strength and timelessness of the "mother nature" as well as its ancient character as a powerful female reigning against the odds. The beeswax sculpture is making the connection to the "mother nature" more tangible as well as transcendent.
Text credit: Tomàš Libertíny, Photo credit: Titia Hahne

New perspectives of making
CRAFT 4.0

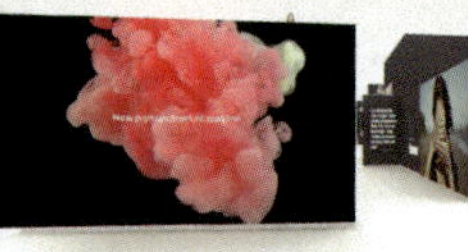

Desig
is th
bridg

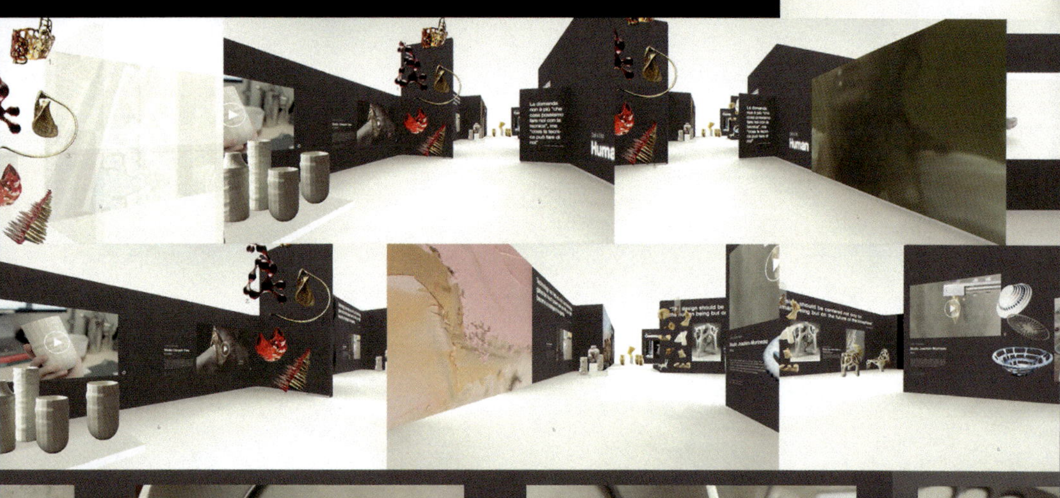

Human
Human

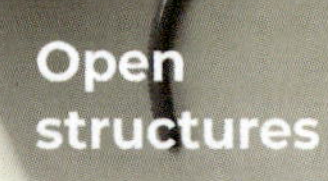

Open
structures

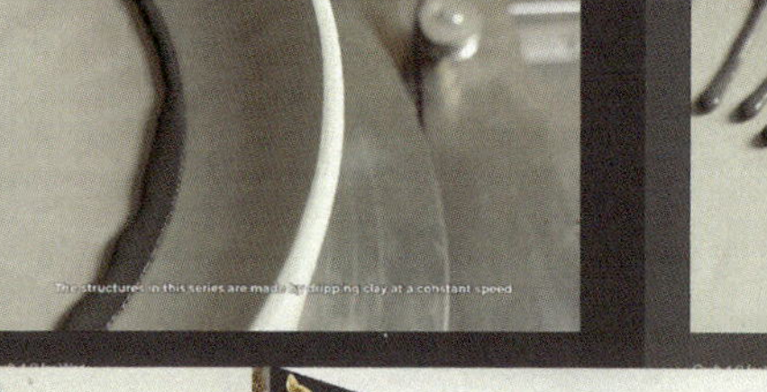

The structures in this series are made by dripping clay at a constant speed

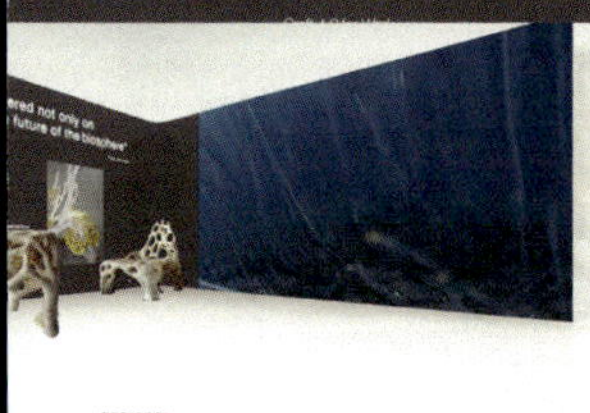

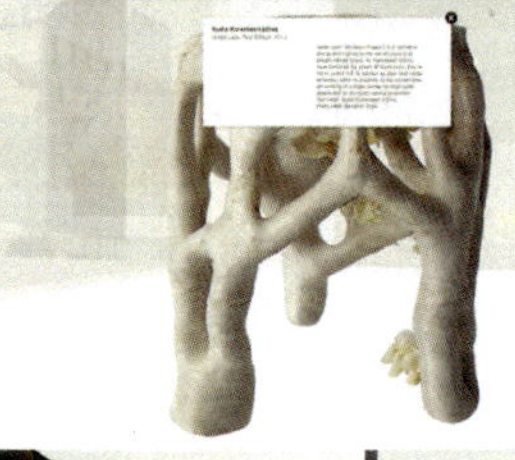

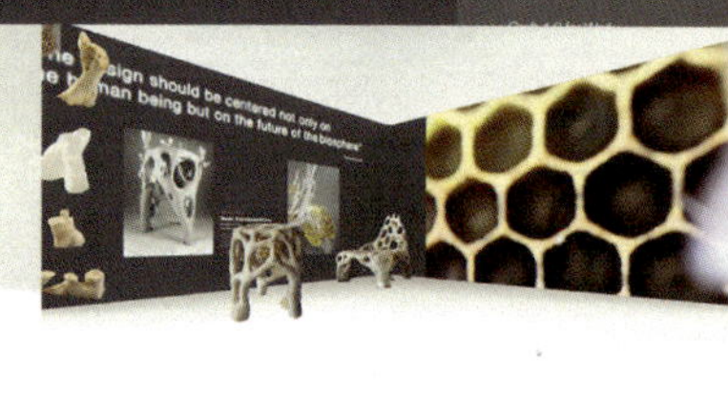

design should be centered not only on
the human being but on the future of the biosphere

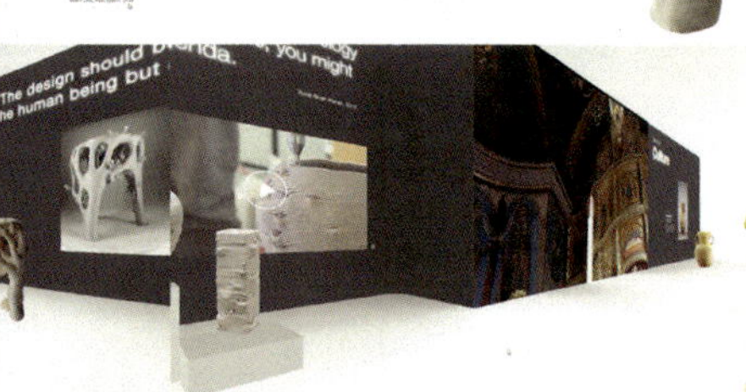

'The design should be centered
the human being but

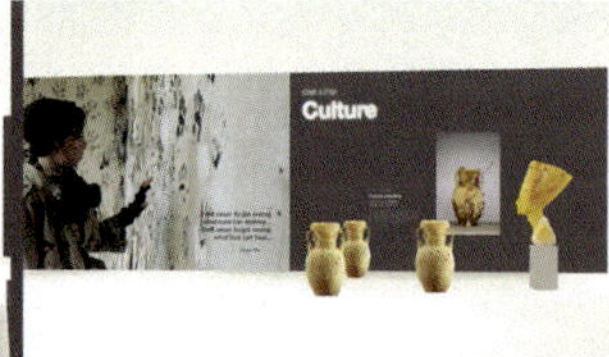

Culture

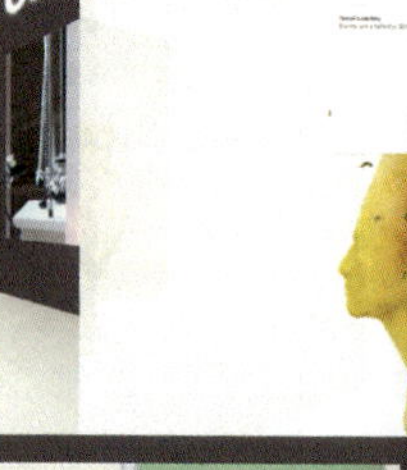

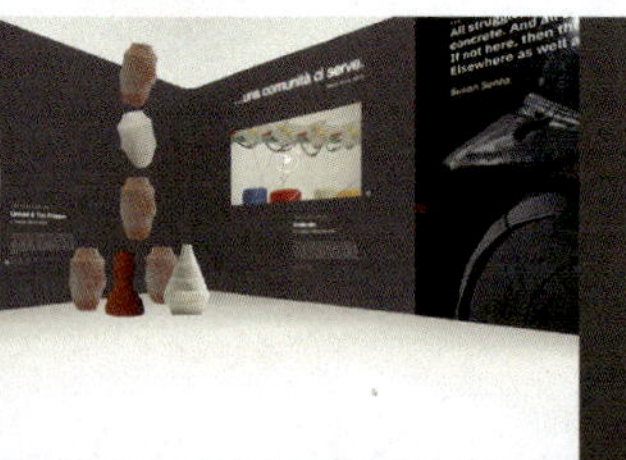

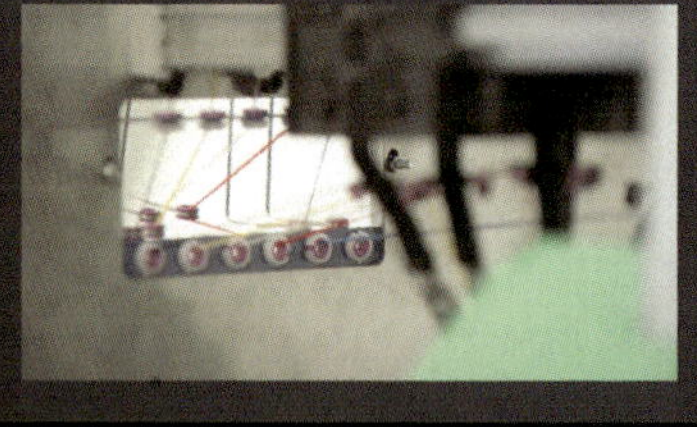

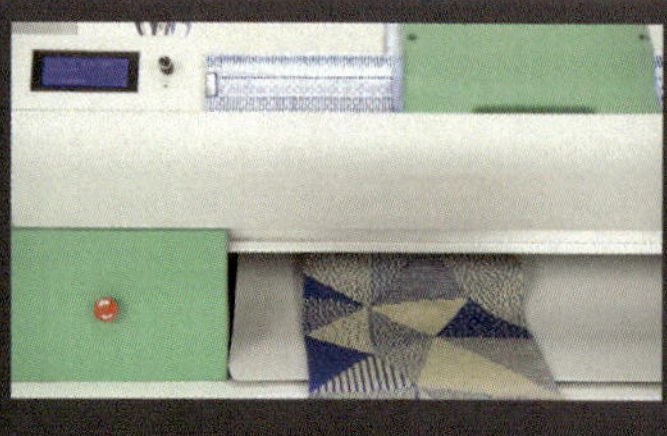

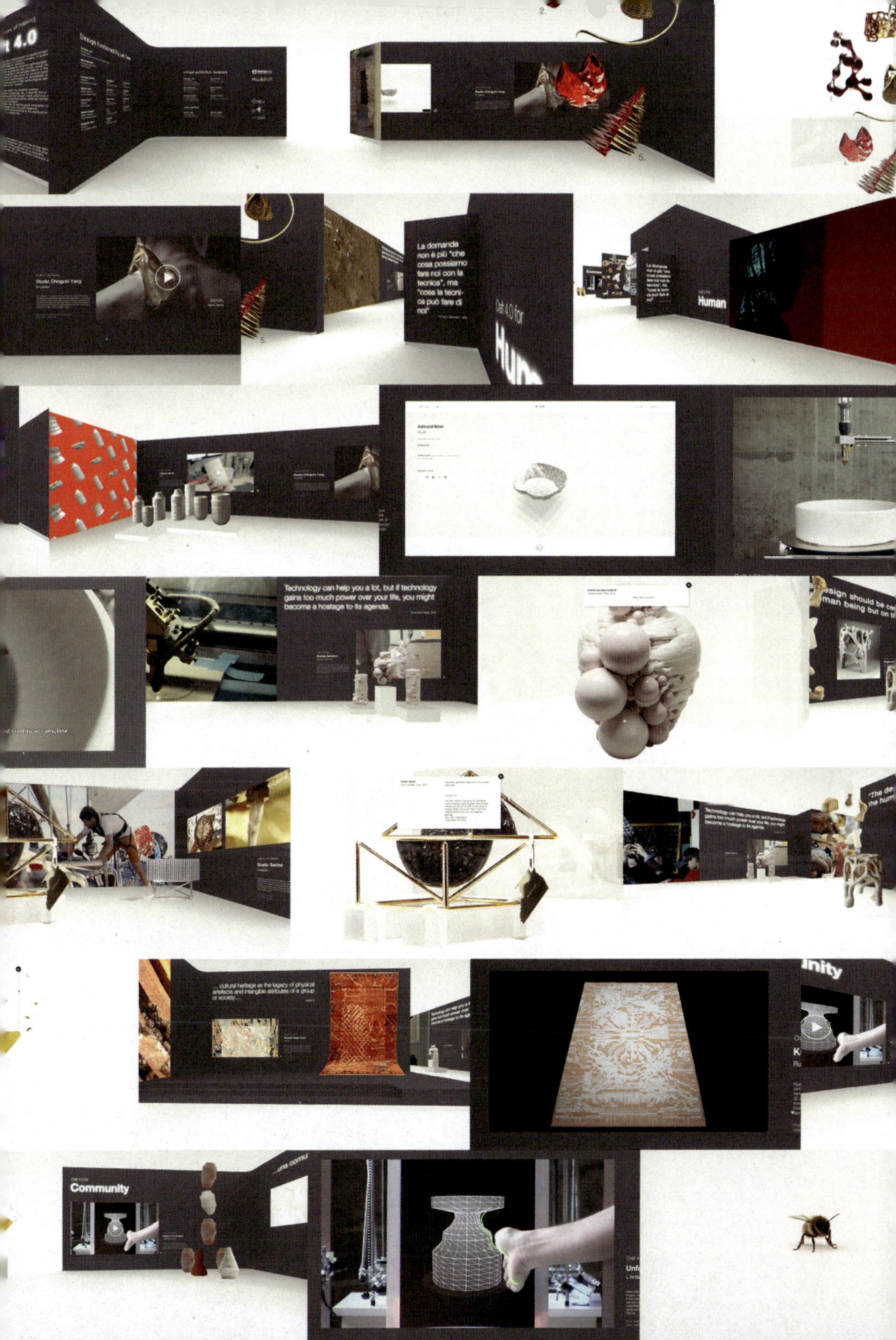

"The question shifts from "what can we do with the technology" to "what can the technology do with us".

Umberto Galimberti

craft 4.0 for

HUMAN

Common Works

Common Works is a design and technology Studio based in London exploring emerging technologies to create anything from online tools for customers, to interactive installations for events. We collaborate closely with clients - ranging from start-ups to global brands - to deliver meaningful, lasting experiences through playful interactions and visual communication. Formed in 2013 by Christopher Waggott, Sam Tripp and Jonny Garrill as a means to experiment across different disciplines and fields, the studio has had the opportunity to work with many companies and institutions, such as Tate Britain, V&A Museum, Somerset House & Atlantic Records.

COMMON WORKS

MIKO

"Miko" is a prototype online platform that allows users to design unique hand cast ceramic objects through playful and engaging interactions. Using simple browser based tools, visitors are able to produce three dimensional models from data captured through a collection of different interactions.

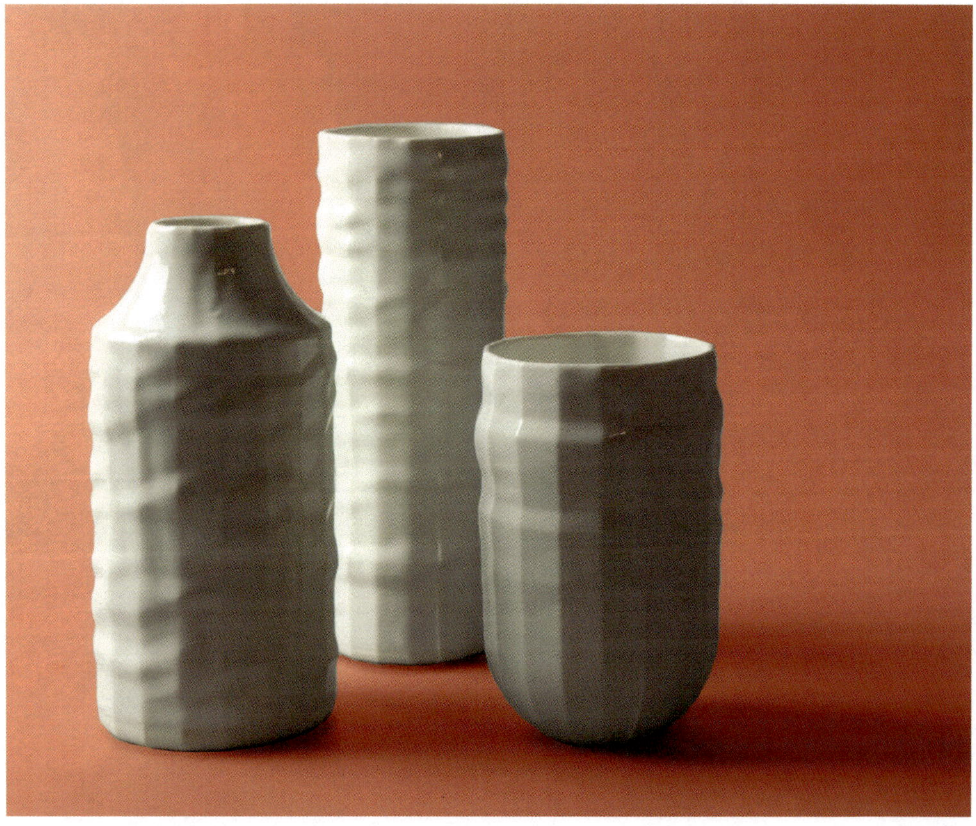

©Common Works

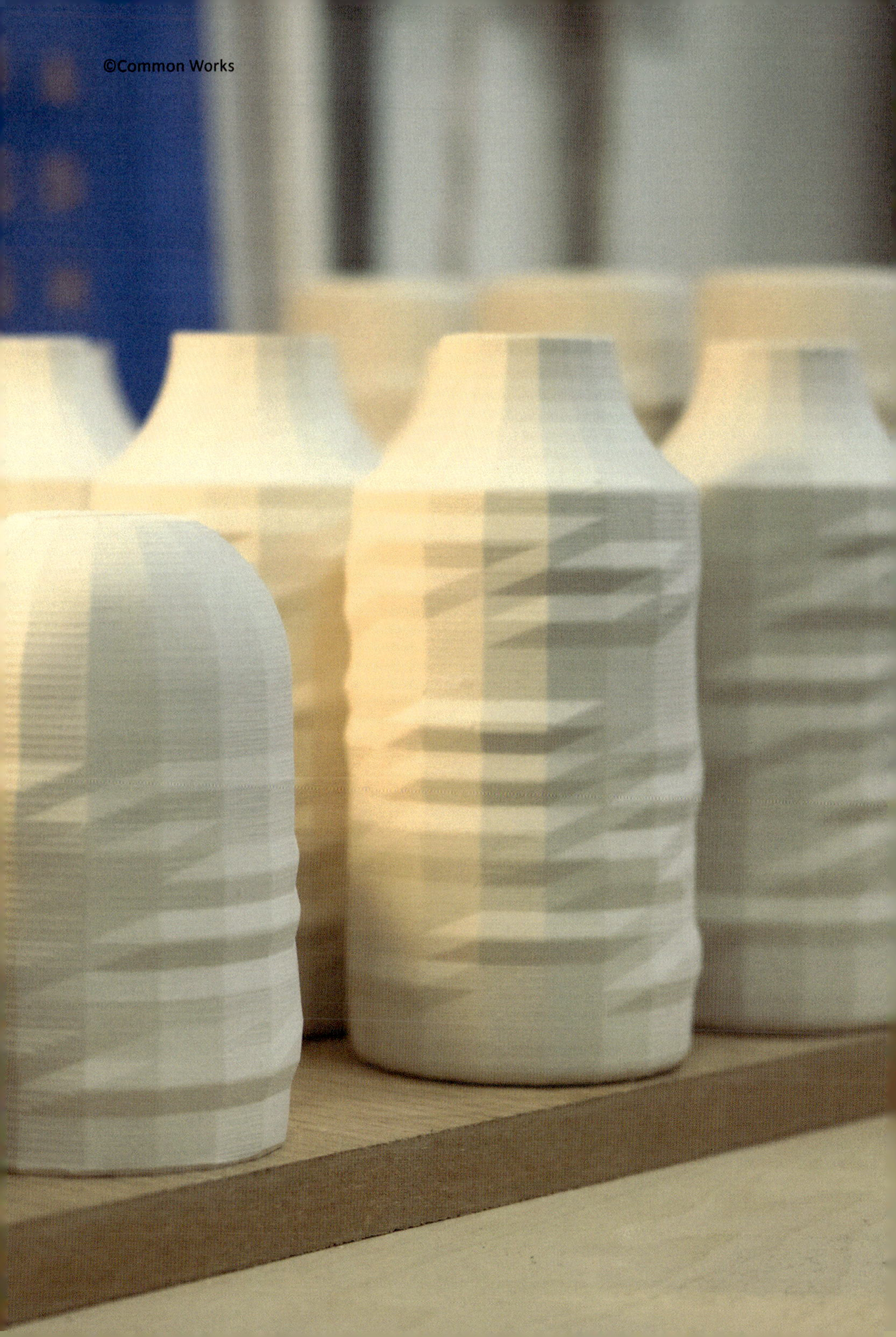

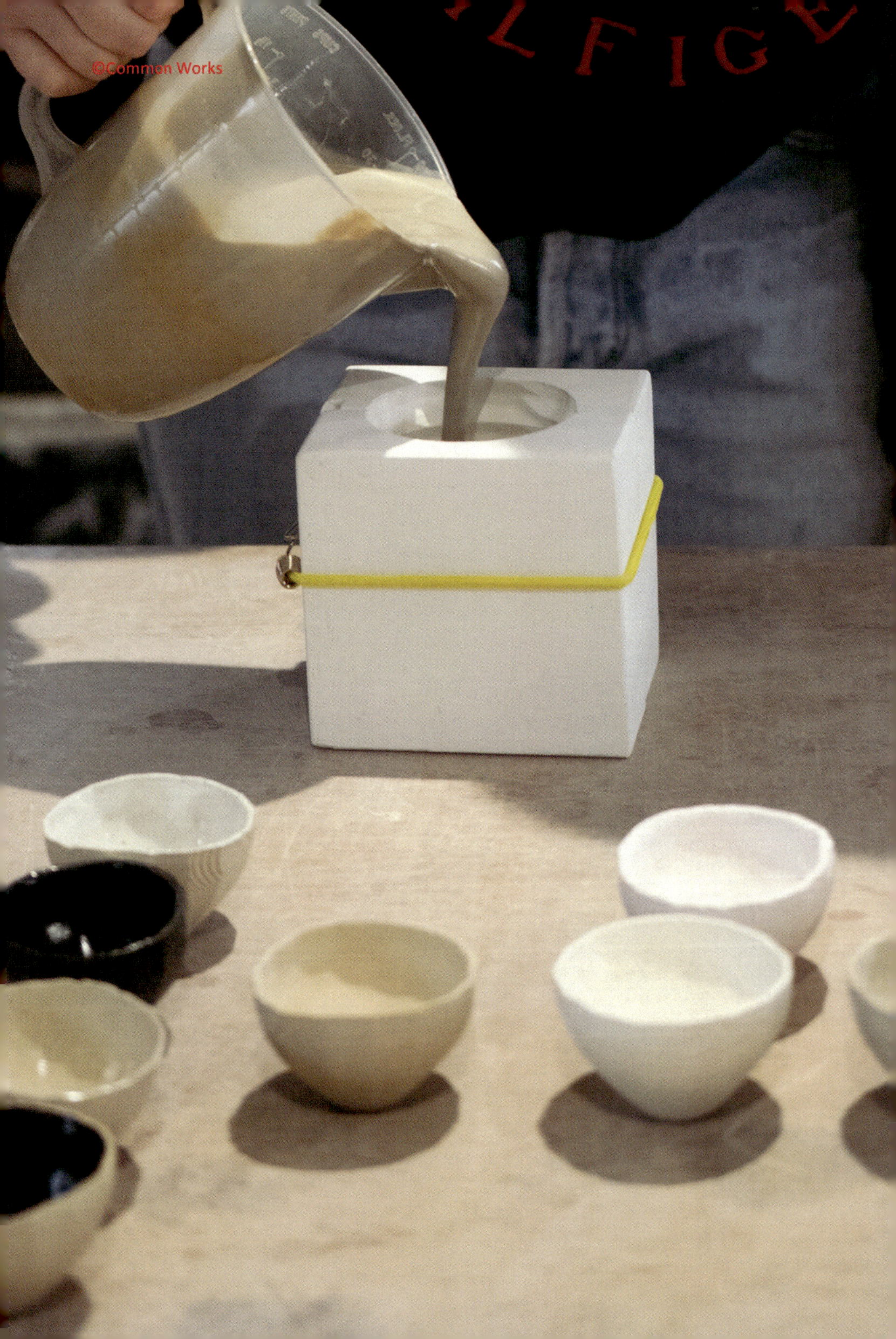

©Common Works

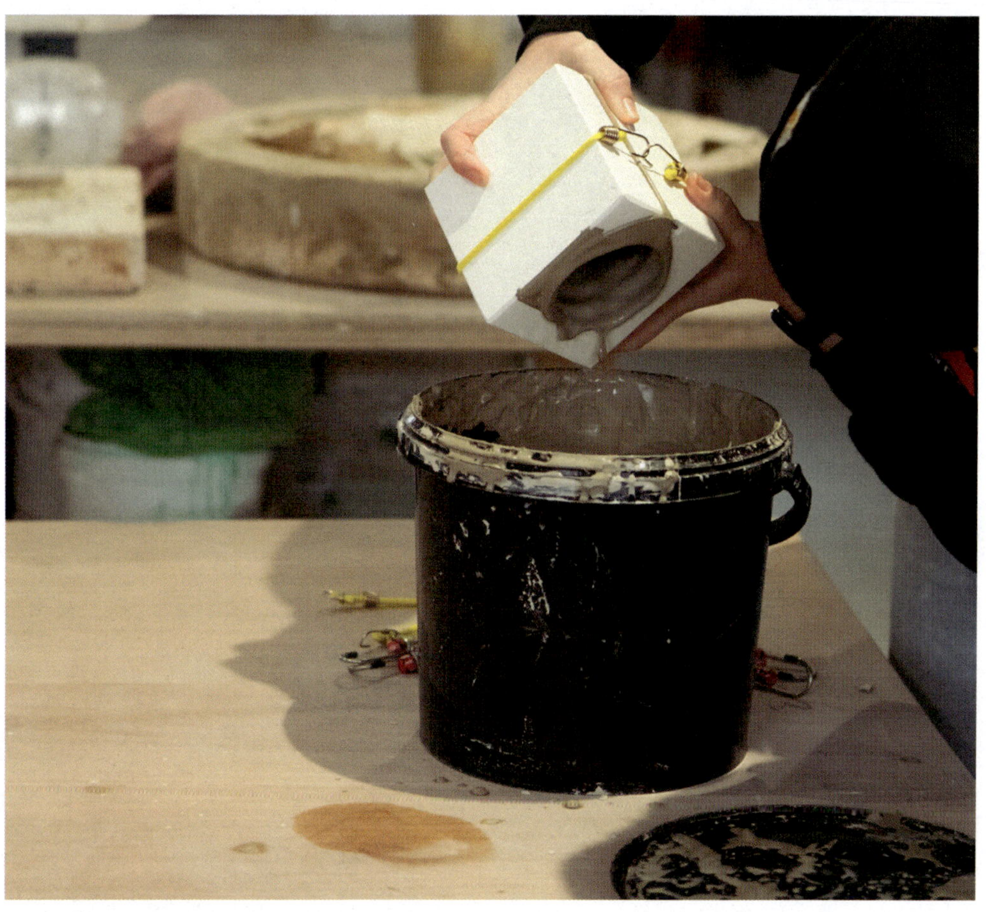

©Common Works

To achieve this, they have utilized unconventional user inputs, such as recording sound from the users' microphone, data from a social media feed and accelerometer data from their phone to help generate a model - resulting in an object that is unique to that visitor. These models are automatically converted into molding machines, ready to be cast and finished using traditional ceramic casting.

Text by: Common Works

Ching-Hui Yang

Studio Ching-Hui Yang is a contemporary jewelry studio based in Amsterdam. Taiwanese designer Ching-Hui Yang is eager to explore different materials, skills and modes to challenge the boundaries of what defines jewelry. She believes jewelry can be a way of communicating emotion between people. For the long term goal, she would like to document and visualize emotion itself - for example, a feeling such as denial, anger, bargain, depression or shame. For this process and the resulting art pieces, her aim is to rethink the definition of empathy.

CHING-HUI YANG

IM-PERFECT

This collection is concerned with the acceptance of acquired physical disability and social attitudes towards personal appearance. The project has used the combination of digital innovation and handcrafting through the use of 3D printing and hand-made finishes.

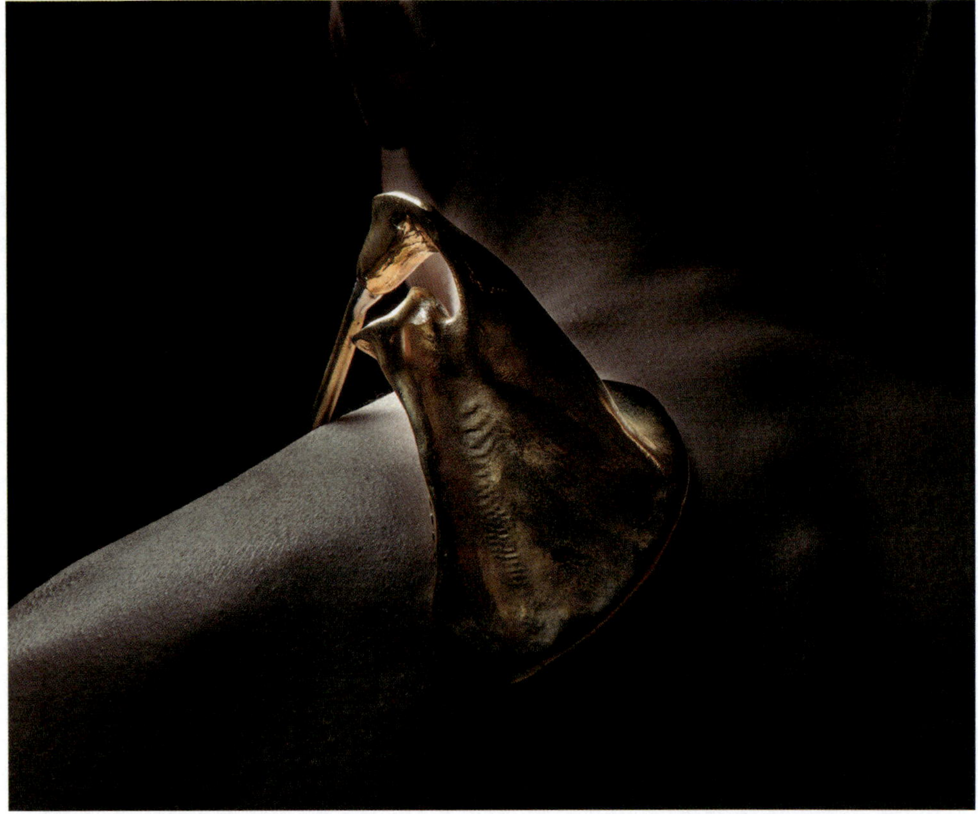

©VC Media Ltd (Vincent Cui Studio)

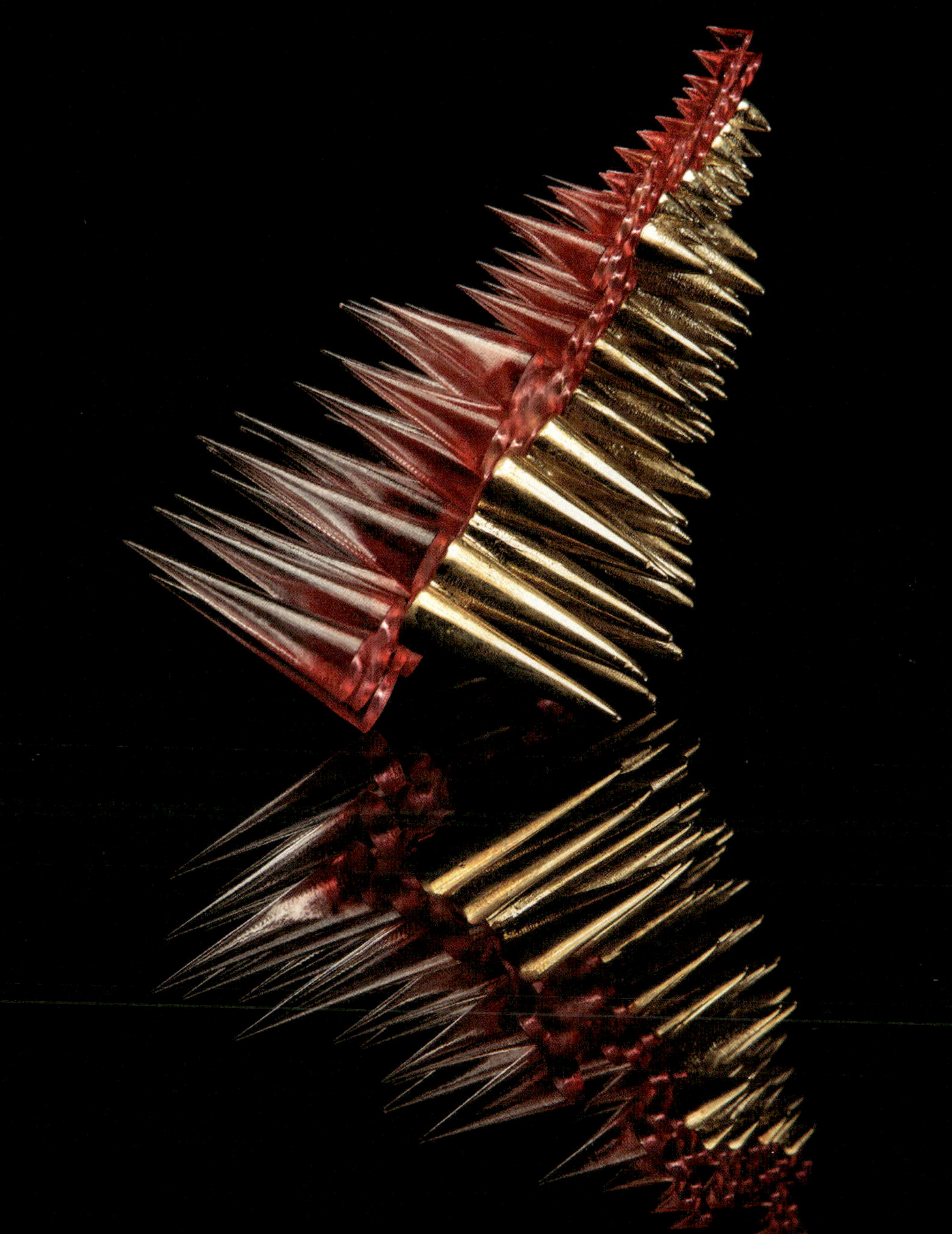
©VC Media Ltd (Vincent Cui Studio)

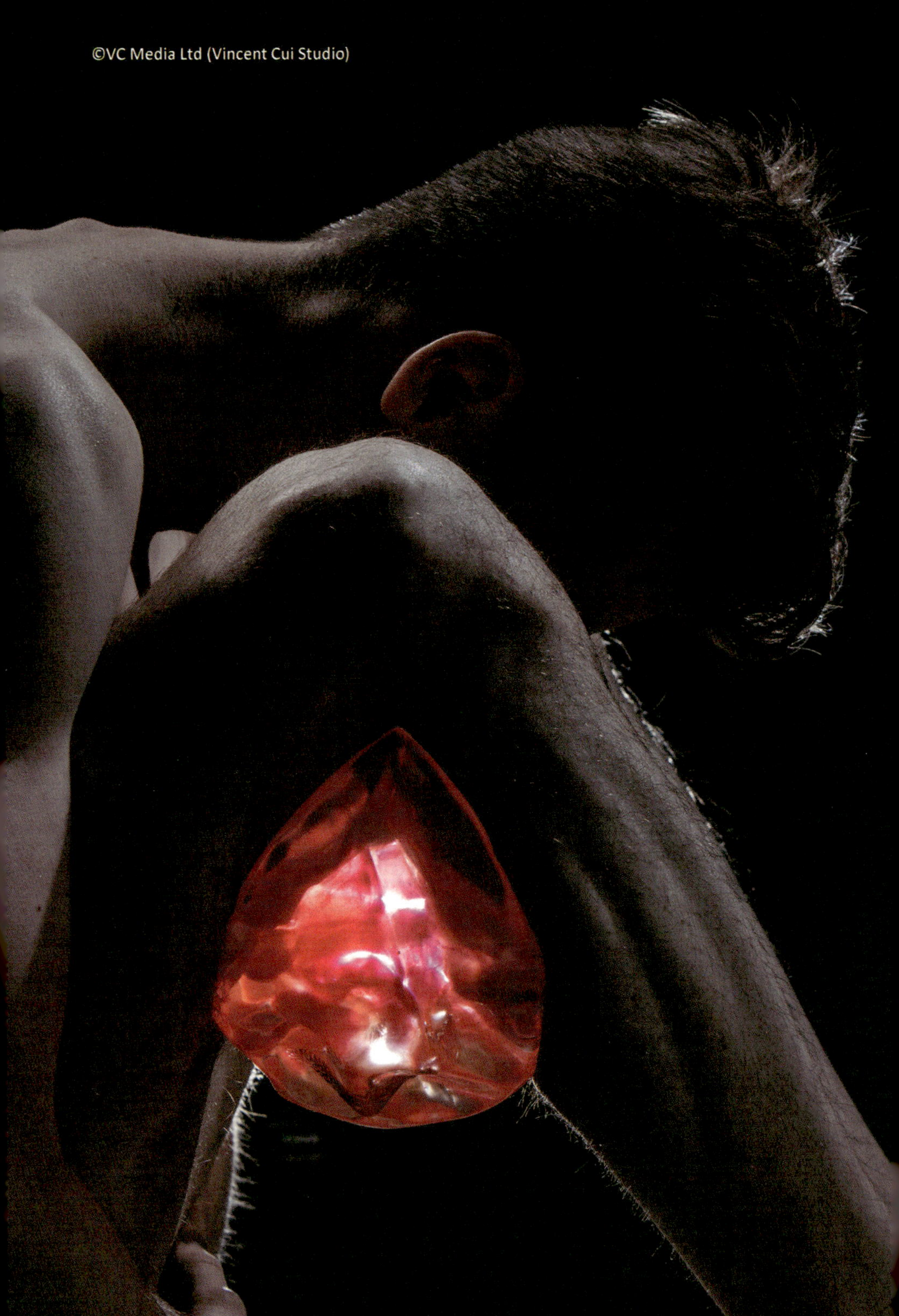
©VC Media Ltd (Vincent Cui Studio)

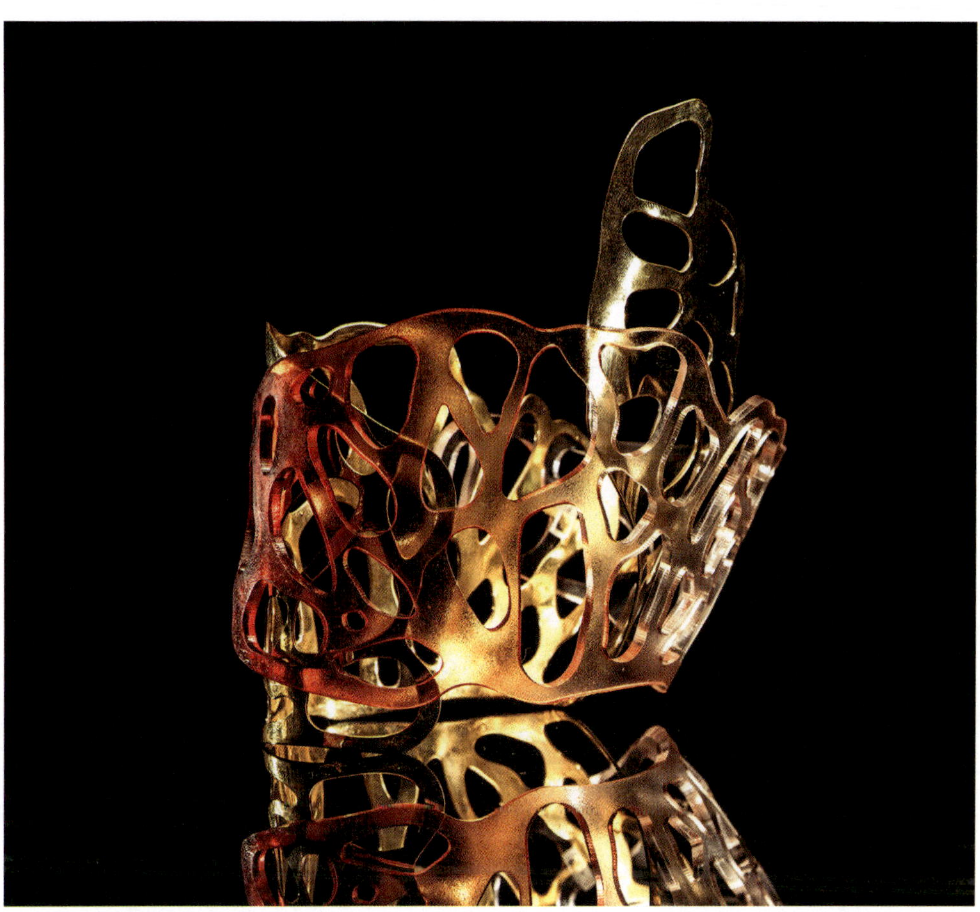

The process of psychosocial adjustment, following an acquired disability, has been viewed as a sequence of stages, similar to those experienced during the grief associated with one's imminent death or the loss of a loved one. The five stages of the Kübler-Ross stage model are the best-known description of the emotional and psychological responses that many people experience when faced with an illness or a life-changing situation. Chinghui Yang's hope is to change the way that people perceive disability and to enable people to empathize with the experience of others who have a disability.

Text by: Ching-Hui Yang

TALK-live transcript

ELEONORA D'ASCENZI: So now we can move on to the next designer studio, Ching-Hui Yang. Ching-Hui, thank you for being here today. Ching-Hui Studio is a contemporary jewelry studio based in Amsterdam. Her project is a part of the human section of the exhibition since she believes that jewelry could be a way to communicate emotions among people. Her project "Im-perfect" proves this. The collection is concerned with the acceptance of the acquired disability by showing five different steps, each represented by different pieces of jewelry. Moreover, she uses both design and digital techniques. Ching-Hui, please tell us more about your project.

CHING-HUI YANG: Thank you. Hi everyone and thanks for inviting me to join the designers' talk. I am Ching-Hui and I am the founder of the studio Yang. I graduated in Material Futures at Central Saint Martins, and after my graduation, I moved to Amsterdam to set up my jewelry studio in 2019. I have always got a lot of inspiration from investigating people's behavior. I believe I can use experimental jewelry as a way to challenge the boundary of therapy design.

For the long-term goal, I would like to document and visualize emotion itself, and through this process, I hope people could rethink the definition of empathy.

Today, I will talk about one of the collections: "Im-perfect". The beginning of the inspiration was given by my aunt: she had polio when she was a child, and she spent the rest of her life in a wheelchair. She told me that it took a long time to get used to accepting her appearance. The first stage of grief is the description of the emotional responses that many people experience when they have the illness. And coincidently, no matter if people have a disability or if they do not, they may face these five stages when people experience a life-changing event. So, I designed a collection of jewelry pieces based on five stages of grief that encourage empathy and allow us to embrace and experience diversity. At the beginning of the research, I have created around 50 different textures and asked around 50 people which emotion they associate with texture.

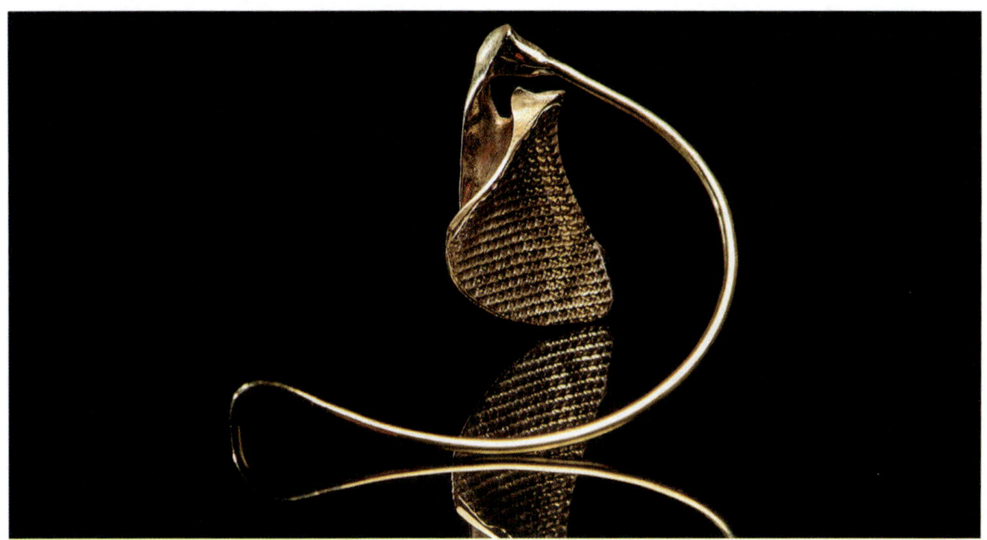

Image 1
©VC Media Ltd (Vincent Cui Studio)

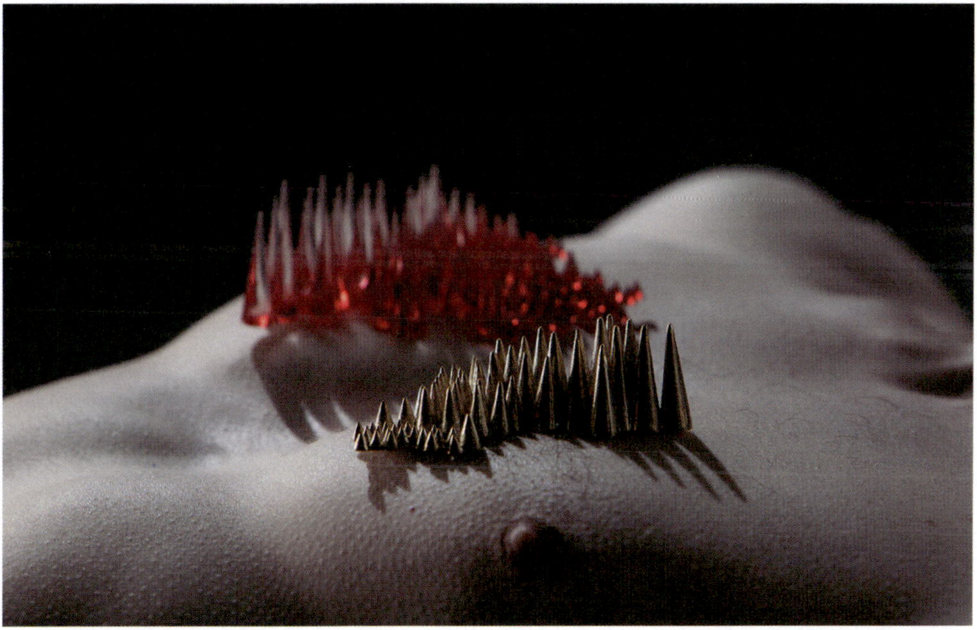

Image 2
©VC Media Ltd (Vincent Cui Studio)

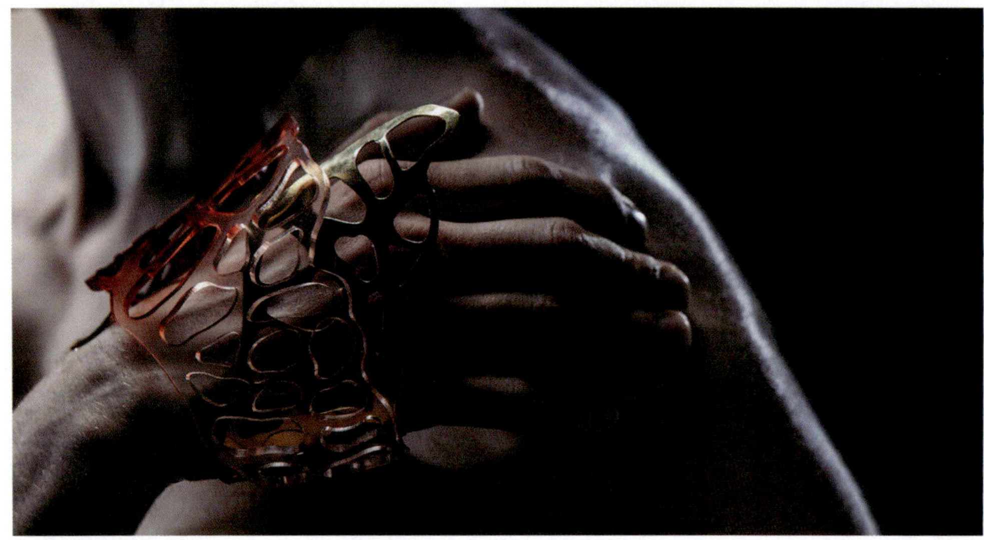

Image 3
©VC Media Ltd (Vincent Cui Studio)

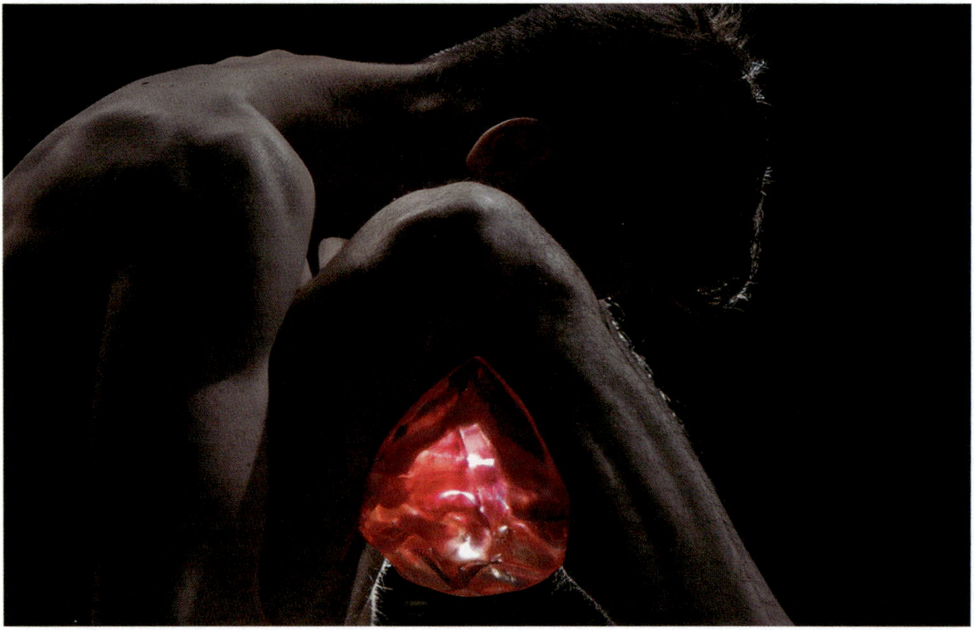

Image 4
©VC Media Ltd (Vincent Cui Studio)

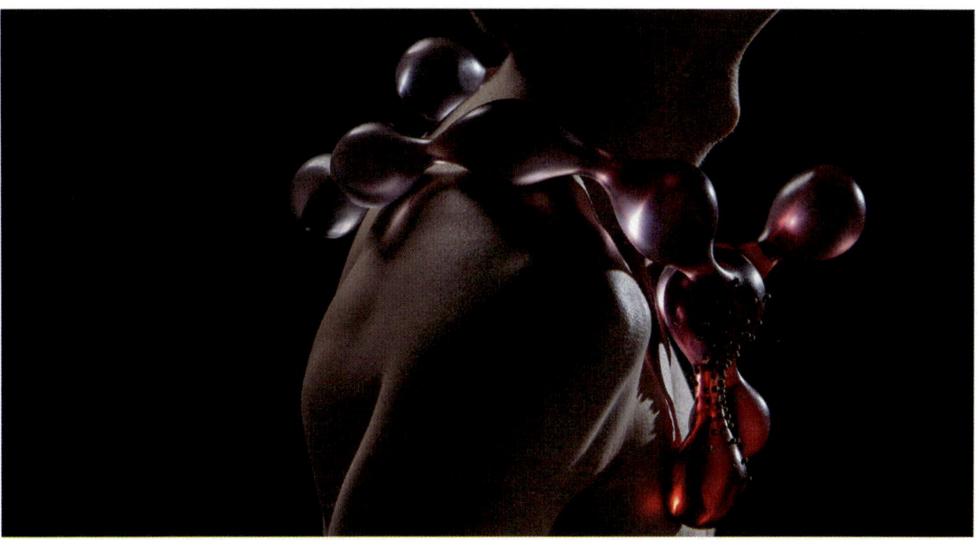

And from the result of the survey, I have created a series of jewelry pieces based on the concept of the five stages of grief. Denial is the first stage, it is usually a temporary defense that will be replaced by partial acceptance. This necklace (Image 1) is inspired by the first stage: denial. I made it by casting brass.

Anger is the second stage of grief when the first stage of denial cannot be maintained any longer and it is replaced by the feeling of anger. This double-side object (Image 2) is inspired by those that can stage anger and is made by casting brass and 3D printing.

The bargain is the third stage of grief. People will try to negotiate their way out from hurting. So, the object (image 3) is inspired by bargains and is made of laser-cut acrylic and laser-cut brass. So, after bargaining, you might go through a stage of depression, you might feel empathy and grief will enter your life at a deeper level. So, this piece (Image 4) is inspired by depression and I casted it in brass.

Moreover, some people said that after the third stage - the bargain - most of the people will enter a depression stage, but some of them will enter the shame stage. So, this necklace (Image 5,6) is inspired by another fourth stage: shame. It has been made by 3D printing.

You might notice I didn't make the last stage: acceptance. I have implied it in every piece. When you go through each stage, you start to accept yourself.
ELEONORA D'ASCENZI: Thank you Ching-Hui for your fascinating vision and also for the touching story and concept idea.

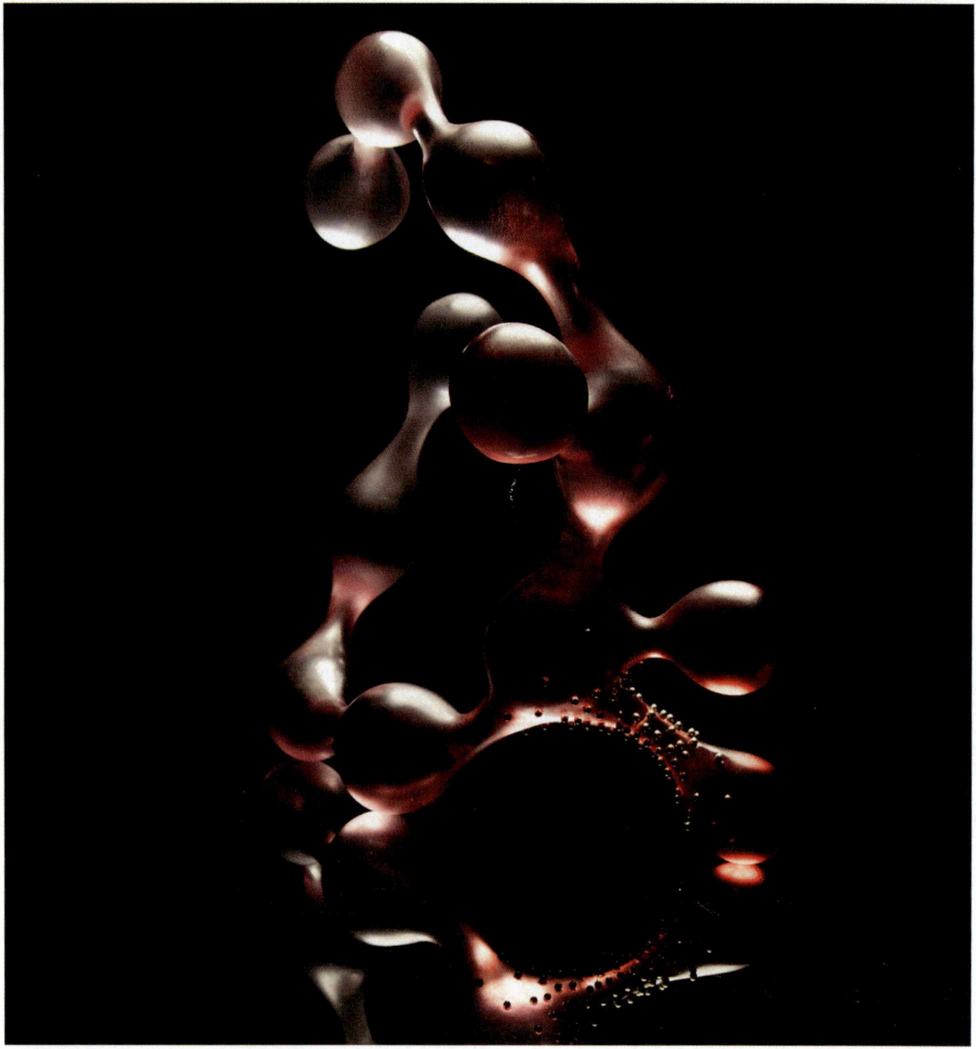

Image 6
©VC Media Ltd (Vincent Cui Studio)

ELEONORA D'ASCENZI: I have some questions for you, Ching-Hui Yang. In the Q&A box, I have asked you if you have any future projects about this theme and how design could help to share emotions among people.

CHING-HUI YANG: For now, I am working on a new project called F.O.G Project… I want to build an emotional library. So, for this project, I am using the AR survey that I have sprayed on my website so that people can join it. I have already gathered around 200 people to join the survey and I have put this outcome to the first collection of F.O.G.

Regarding the second question, at the beginning of the project, during the design phase, I just thought it was a design project. But when I exhibited in the Dutch Design Week and I explained my project, I remembered some people who have a diagnosis of cancer, someone divorced, and when I explained every piece to them, they started to cry and then explained what they went through. At the same time, I feel like I can help people. I think no one has perfect mental health all the time but, in this world, where people are asked to be mentally well, I feel harsh for everyone. A lot of people didn't talk about it, and I feel a bit sad about all this, actually. I hear a statement from Un (Image 6) which says, "the basic challenge is always the stigma of mental health". People always believe that society will avoid communicating with people who have mental issues. So, I feel inspired by the Dutch Design. I love feedback from the audience and that is why I continue to do emotional therapy things. For this new project, I want to create an emotion library where people see the project and maybe bring the object to the doctor and say "Oh, actually I cannot explain what I'm feeling but this object is what I feel right now".

ELEONORA D'ASCENZI: Thank you. I have two more questions for you. What are the objects of "Im-perfect" you are particularly proud of or you feel especially attached to and why? And what are the effects on people wearing jewelry?

CHING-HUI YANG: Yeah. I actually really like my project because before I didn't know how to translate the emotion from scratch to the final outcome. Since my final project in my BA, I told my tutor, "I don't know how to translate the emotion into jewelry pieces and into an outcome". And she said, "Maybe you don't have to. Just ask the people which texture they would associate with which emotion because everyone has their own emotion, no matter who they are. From the result of the survey, you might get some inspiration from them".

"Technology can help you a lot, but if technology gains too much power over your life, you might become a hostage to its agenda.

Yuval Noah Harari

craft 4.0 for

WORK

Studio Joachim-Morineau

Studio JOACHIM-MORINEAU is a design studio founded by Carla Joachim and Jordan Morineau, based in Eindhoven (NL). Their studio is located in an old Philips warehouse reconverted in a workshop with several other designers. From ceramic experiments and research to manufactured metal furniture, their work is a mix of crafts, technology and industrial techniques. Carla and Jordan first worked together during their studies in Paris at ENSAAMA. They moved to the Design Academy Eindhoven and graduated with honors from Man and Activity in 2018. They used their background and experiences to encourage each other to explore/try new things. They aspire to research original techniques and collaborate with artisans and industries from different parts of the world to bring surprising outcomes.

JOACHIM-MORINEAU

MOCA

"Moca" is a ceramic research based on a dripping machine. The project comes from the idea of combining technology and craft with a human/natural touch. The machine drips liquid porcelain/earthenware at a certain rhythm which creates a new ceramic language.

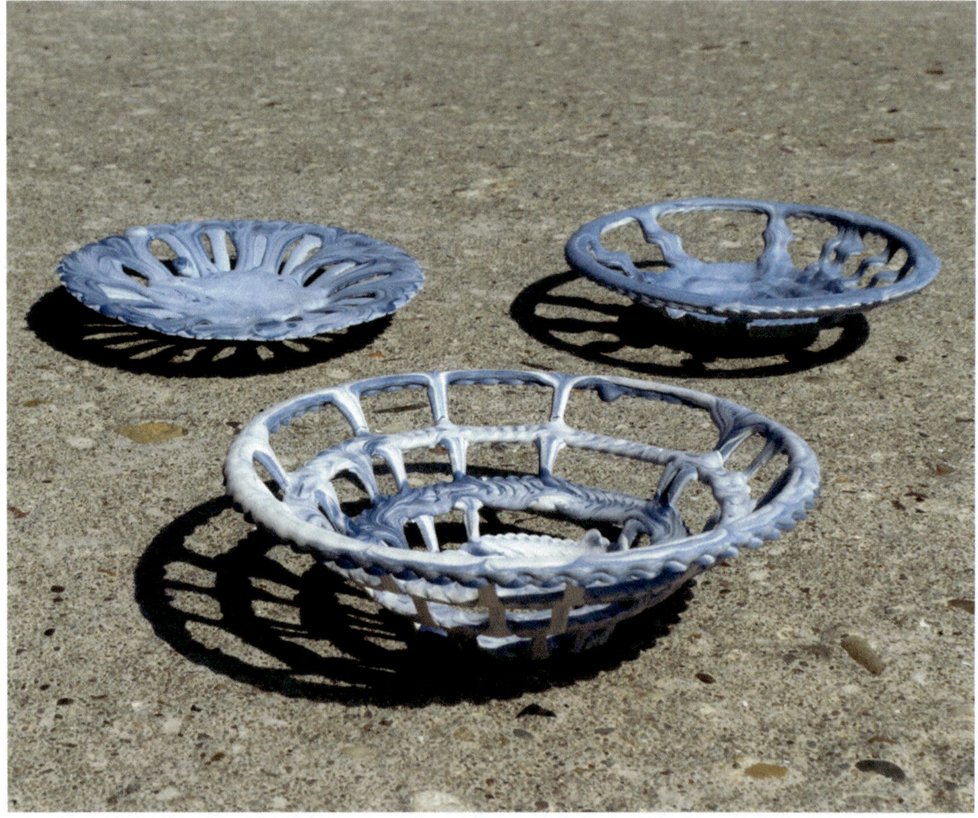

©Pierre Castignola

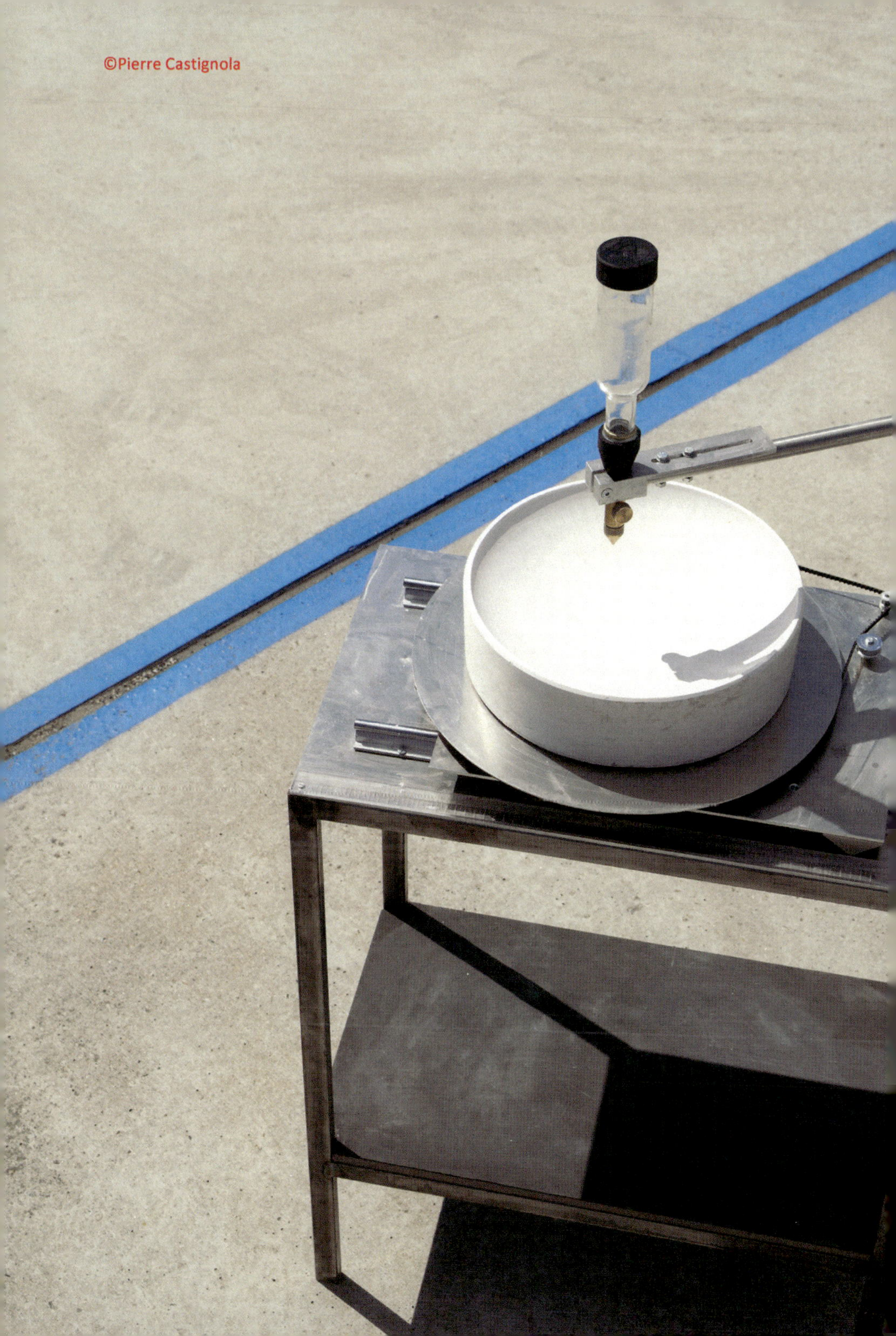

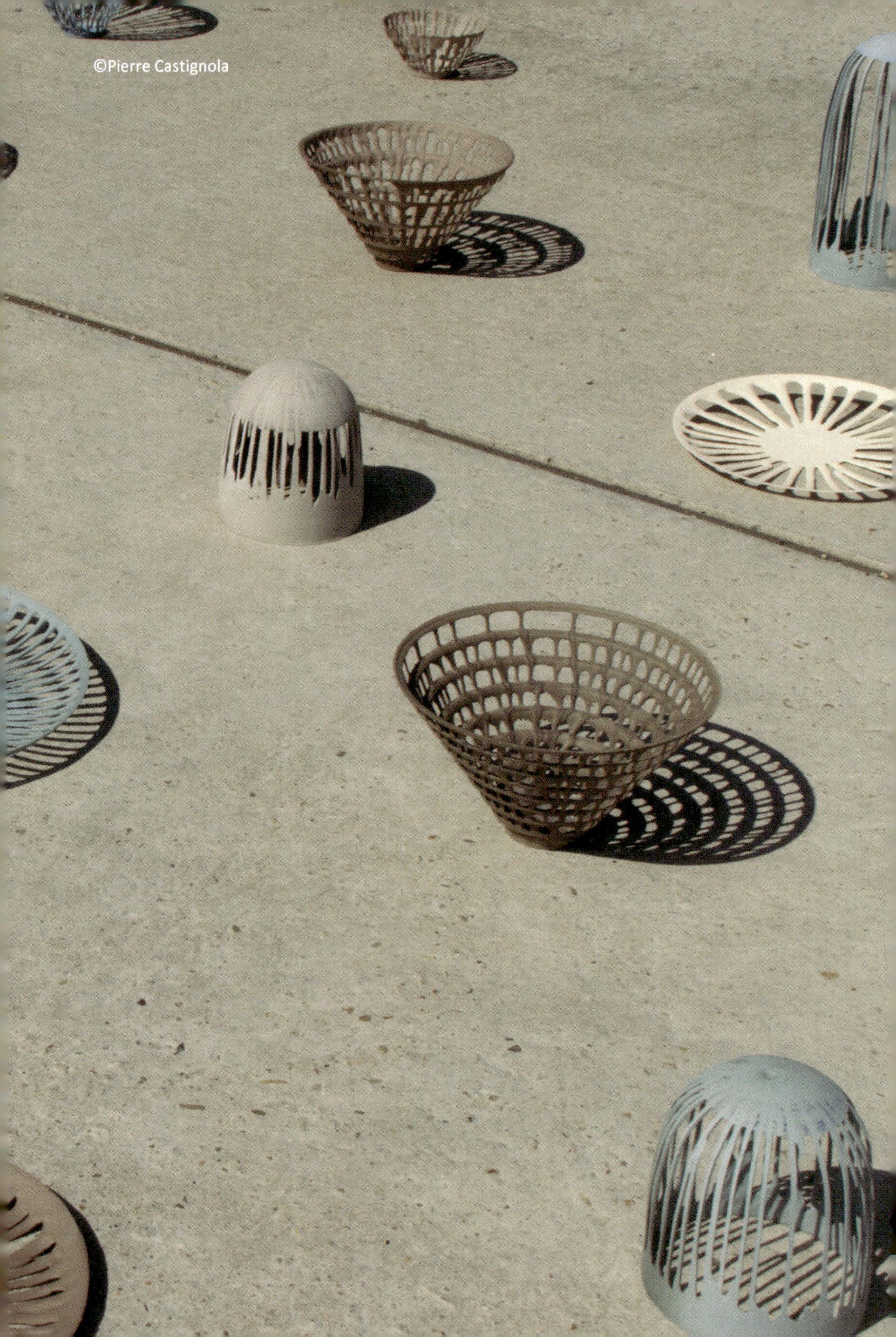
©Pierre Castignola

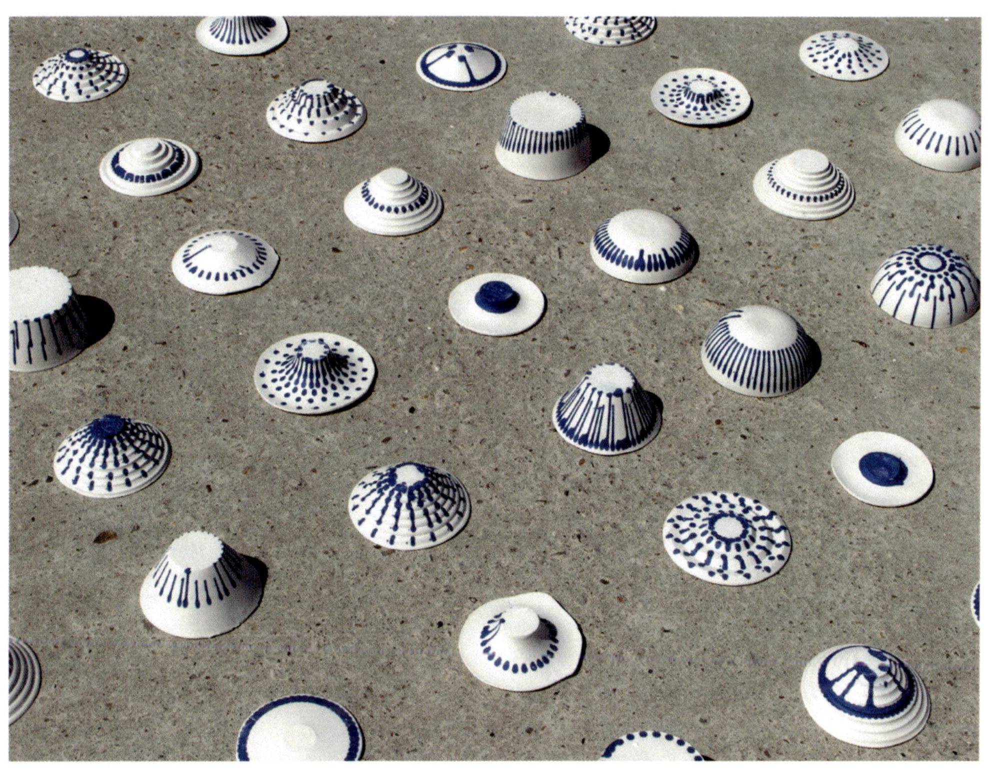

"Moca" is a continuous research where Joachim-Morineau tries to push the boundaries of the ceramic world with an innovative technique. Through the code they created, they can choose the speed and the movements of the platform, and therefore the ceramic outcome. The machine is the link between crafts and industries: they can produce the same object at almost an industrial level, but still each piece is unique.

Text by: Joachim-Morineau

TALK-live transcript

ELEONORA D'ASCENZI: We have the pleasure to have with us JOACHIM-MORINEAU, a design studio based in Eindhoven and founded by Carla Joachim and Jordan Morineau. The studio represents the importance of using technology for craftsmanship through their project, "Moca", that is part of the *Craft 4.0* for work (Image 1) and it was their common graduation project as well as the starting point of the company. Guys, let us know a little bit more about you and your concept idea.
CARLA MORINEAU: Ok I am going to briefly introduce the studio. We are both French, living in the Netherlands, working in Eindhoven, in the beautiful space you can see in this picture (Image 2), a big workshop that we share with other designers. "Moca" is a ceramic research based on a dripping machine we developed. The project comes from the idea of combining technology and craft to create a series of objects with a human/natural touch. It is a continuous investigation where we try to push the boundaries of the ceramic world with an innovative technique. The machine drips liquid clay at a certain rhythm which creates a new ceramic language. The idea we had is more related to a question: due to our product design background, we were interested in the idea of making a product but... how can we make it unique? And after looking into a lot of industrial processes combined with crafts, we designed "Moca", the ceramic dripping machine.
The liquid clay drips through a nozzle with a specific diameter that we can change. The drops fall into a plaster mold placed on a rotating platform which also moves on an X-axis. Everything is controlled by Arduino. Through the code we created, we can choose the speed and the movements of the platform, and therefore the ceramic outcome. The machine is the link between crafts and industries: it can produce the same object at almost an industrial level, but still each piece is unique.

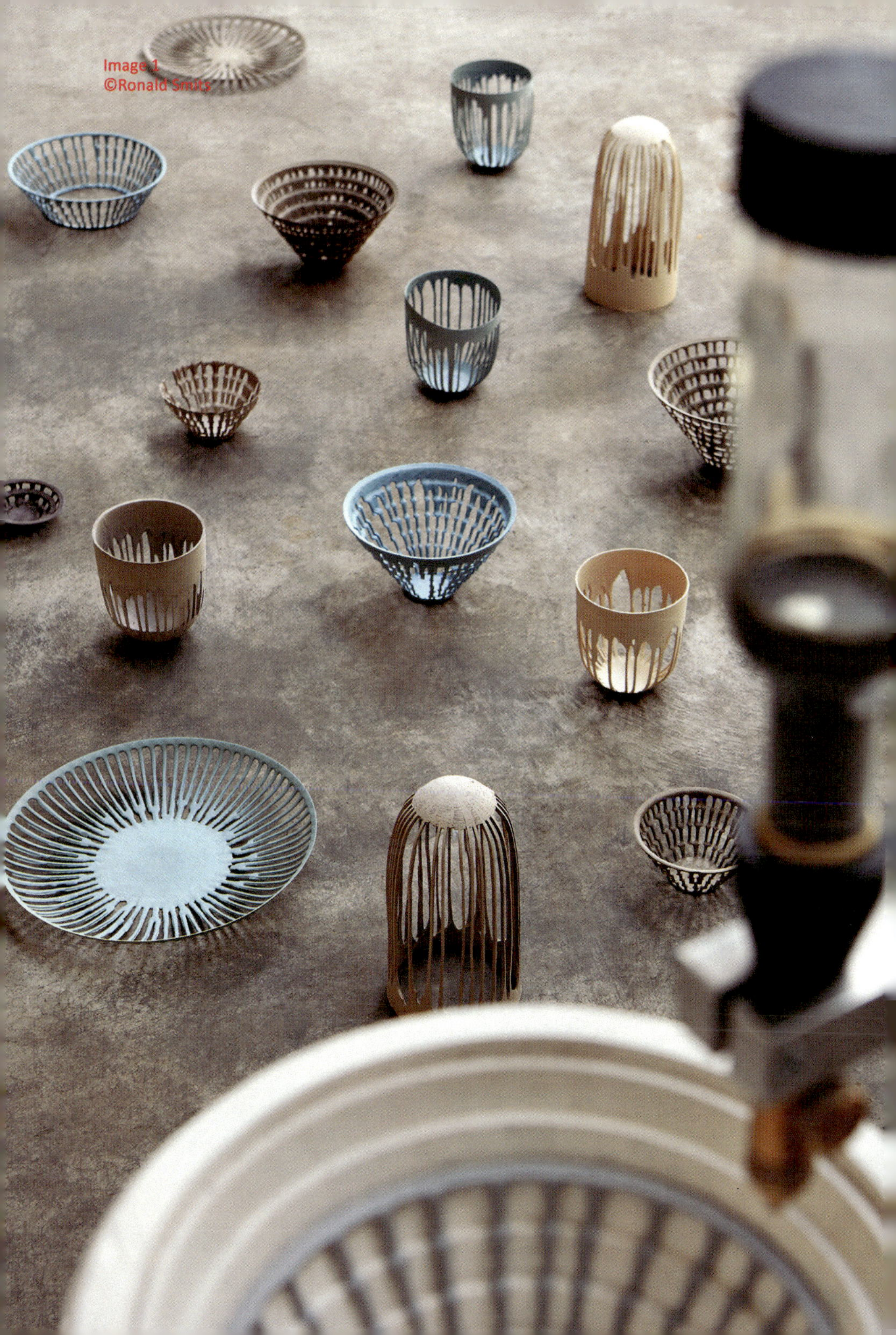
Image 1
©Ronald Smits

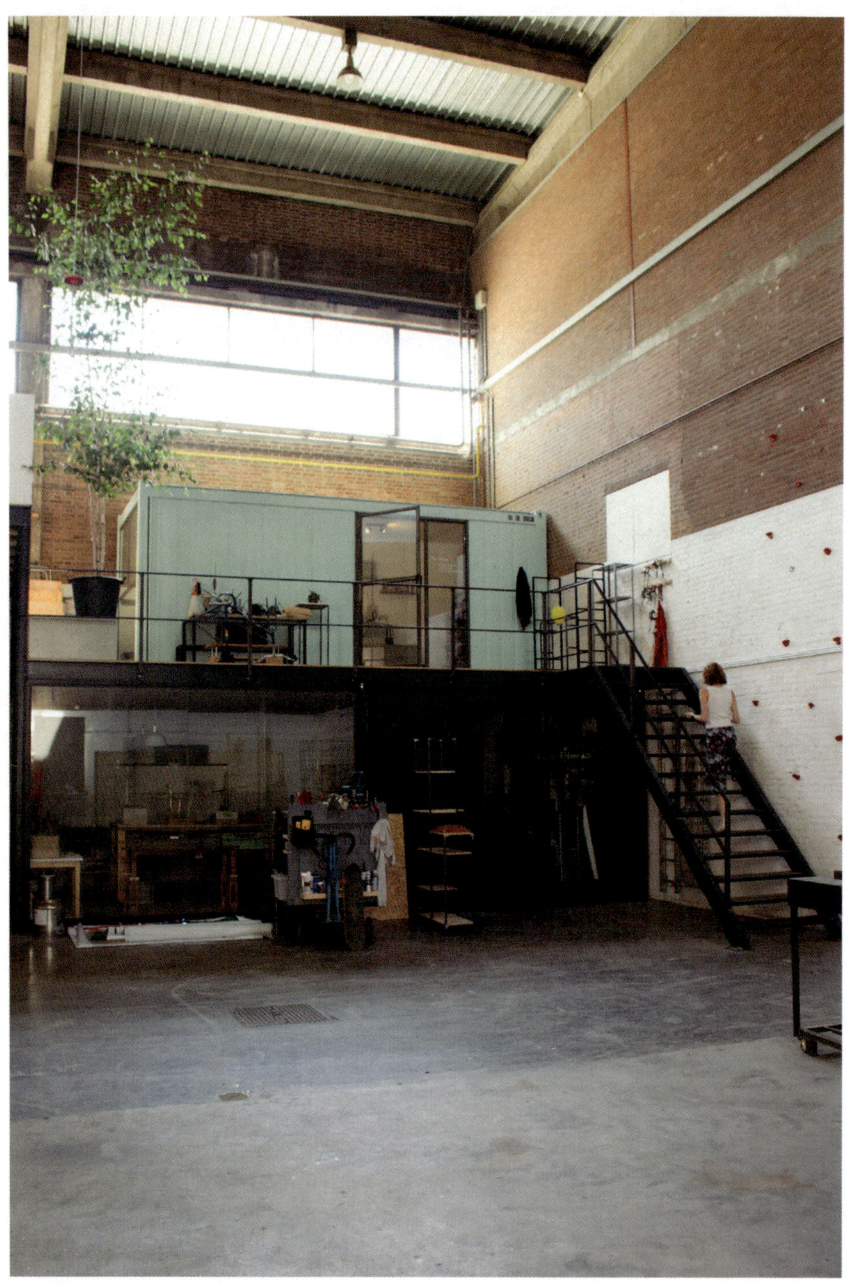

Image 2
©Joachim-Morineau

JORDAN MORINEAU: During our research we have encountered a lot of difficulties and errors. Thus, we had to look into different clays, different materials or stoneware. So, for different graphics and textures, we use different clays. As you can see in the picture (Image 3), we had a lot of tests and not everything worked. But at one point, we could see the pattern where we wanted to go and then we could reproduce it every time.

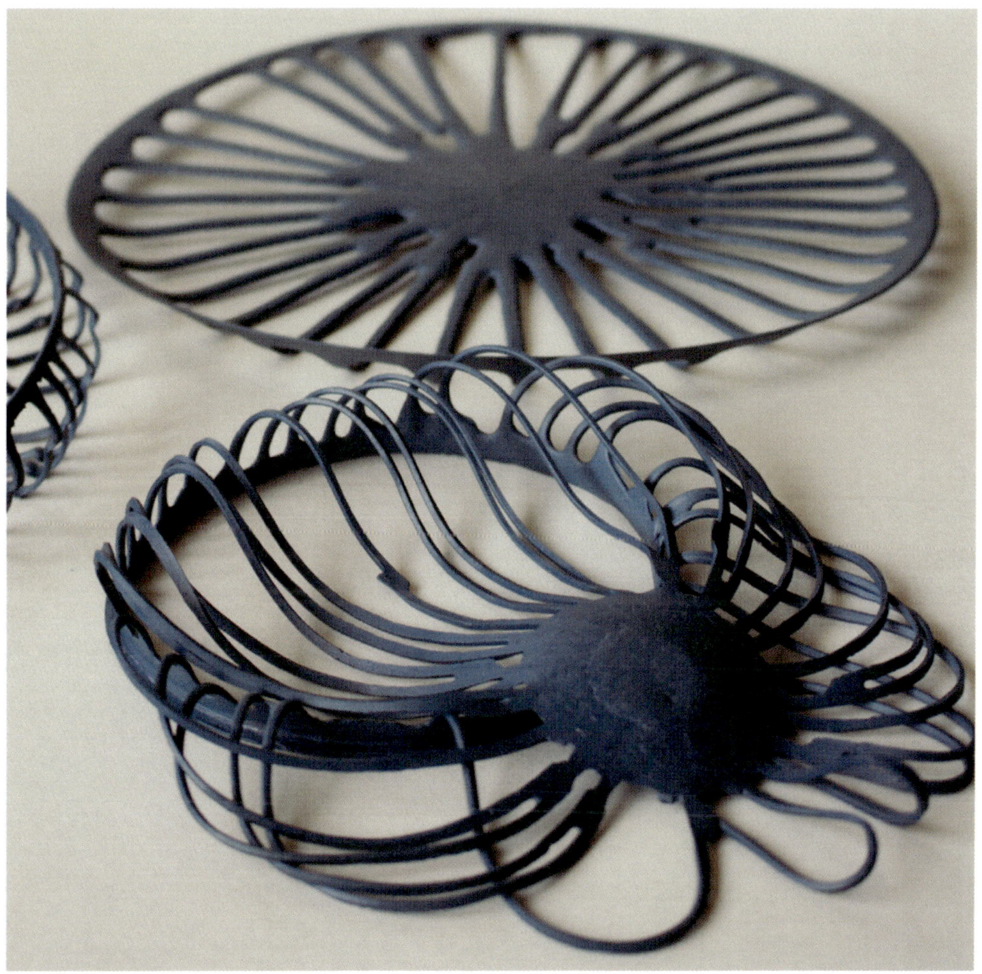

Image 3
©Joachim-Morineau

Moreover, we explored different paths, categorized by:
Textures: the drops left on the mold are covered with a slip clay layer. It creates a texture within the object, only visible on one side (Images 4,5,6,).
Open structures: by combining specific angles of molds, rotation speed and dripping flow, they succeed in building volumes with different types of architectures (Images 7, 8).
Patterns: they researched how the angles and shapes of the molds influence the drops to create various motifs. The graphic outcomes are mathematical. With this process, they can design a pattern in a few seconds within the ceramic (Image 9).
ELEONORA D'ASCENZI: Perfect, thank you for your explanation. It is a very interesting project and thank you also for showing us how technology could represent uniqueness and imperfection.

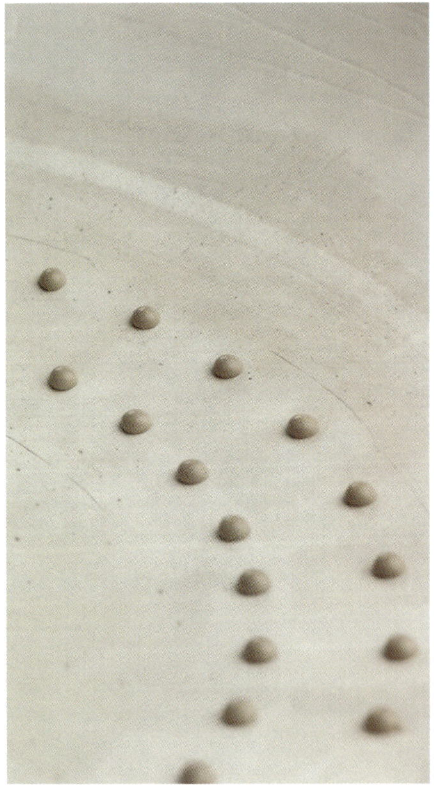

Image 4
©Joachim-Morineau

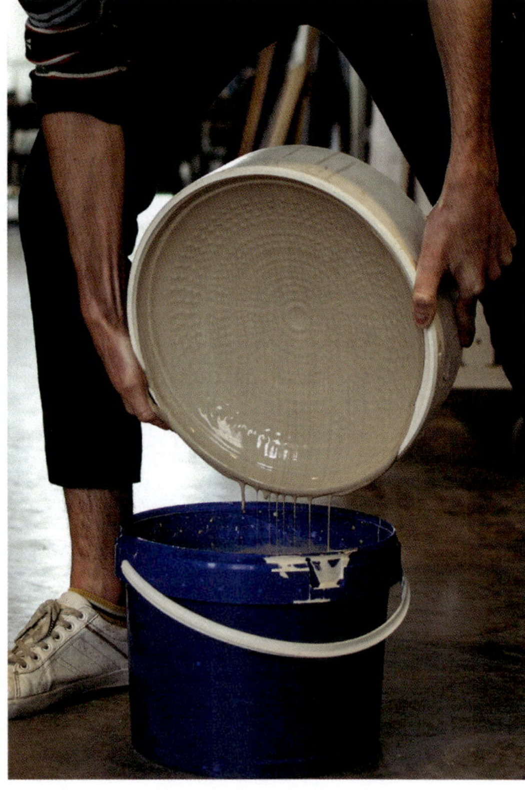

Image 5
©Joachim-Morineau

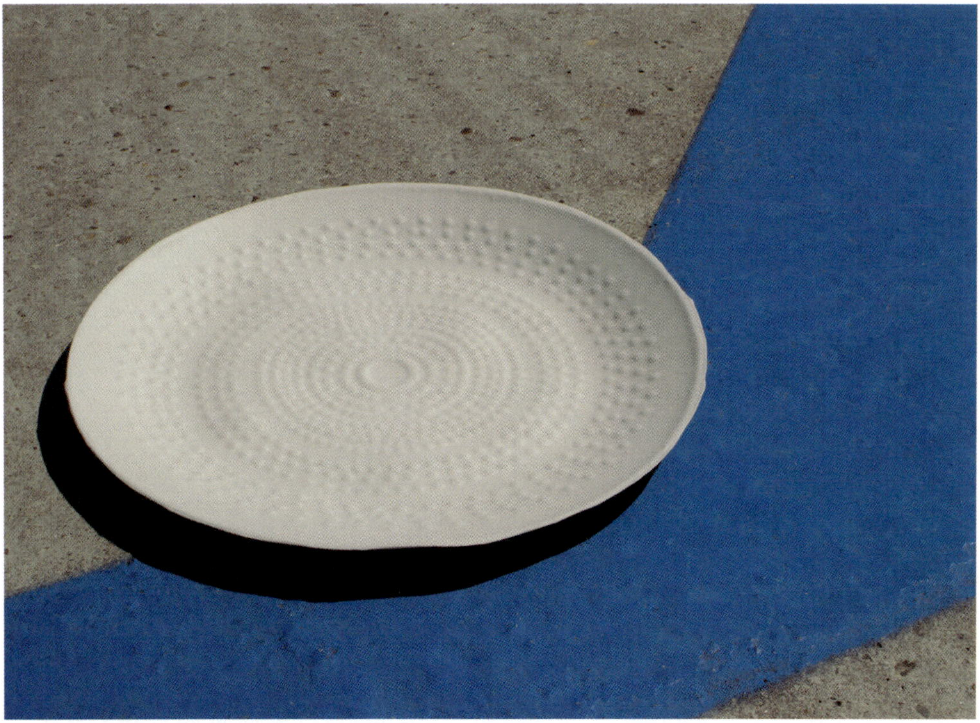

Image 6
©Pierre Castignola

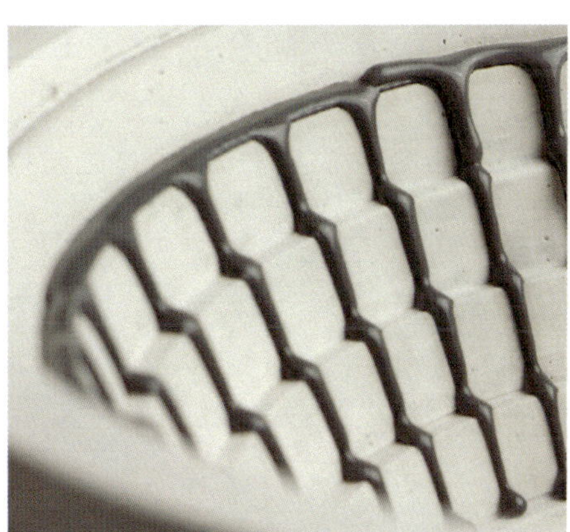

Image 7
©Joachim-Morineau

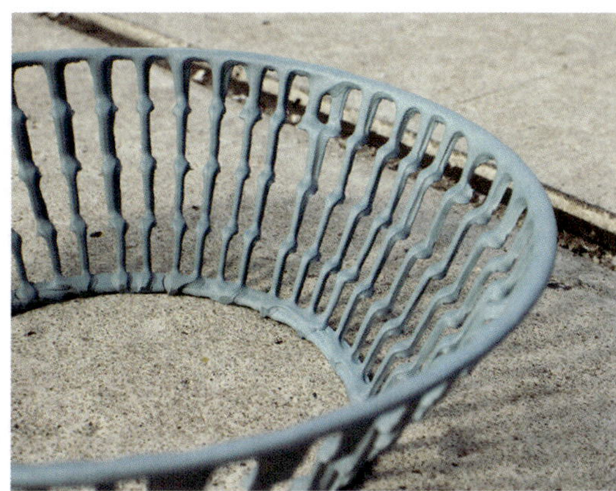

Image 8
©Pierre Castignola

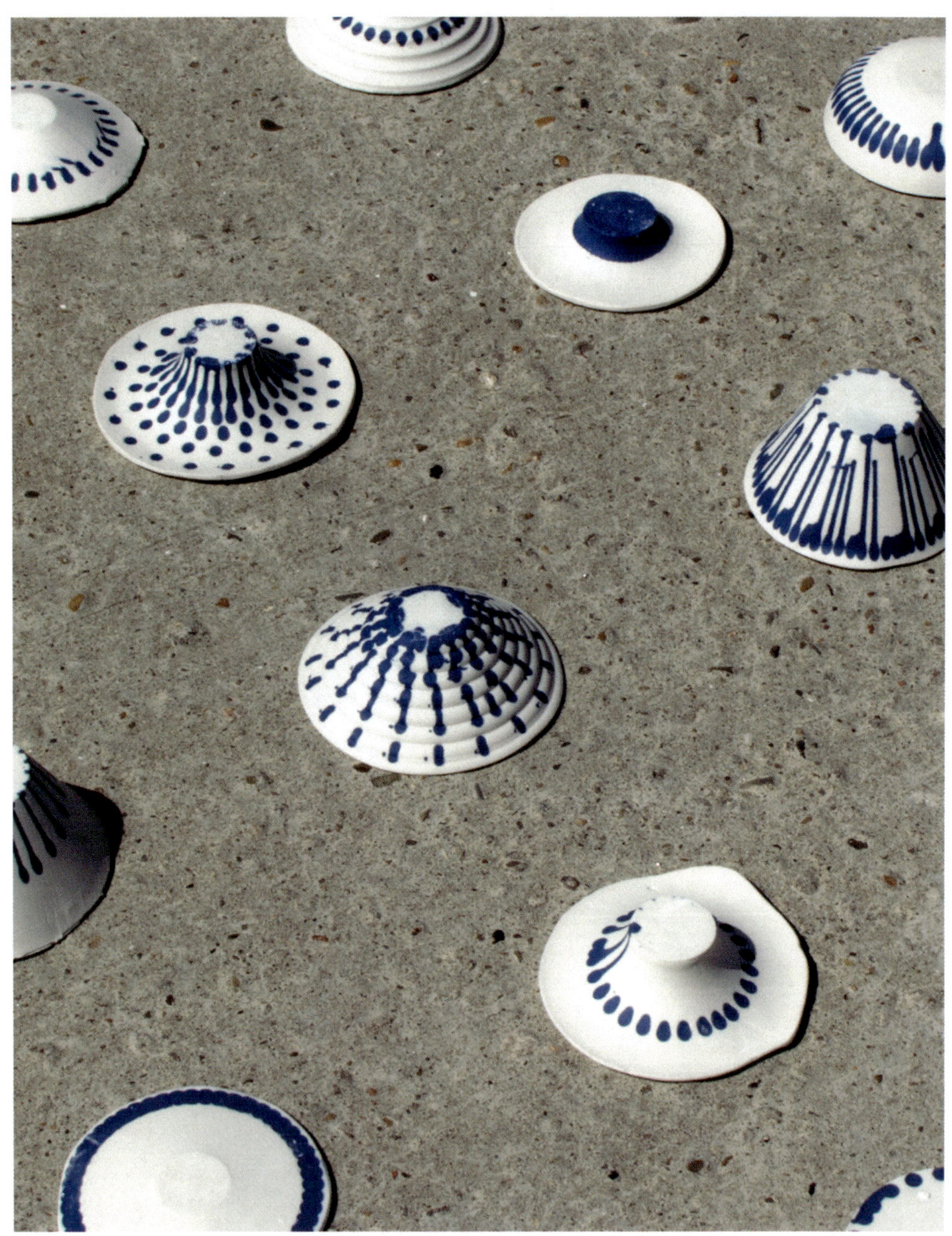

Image 9
©Pierre Castignola

QUESTIONS AND ANSWERS

ELEONORA D'ASCENZI: How did you arrive at the results we see in your research?

JORDAN MORINEAU: Before arriving at this point, we had two different steps. The first one was making the machine work the way we wanted (Images 10,11) The second part was the material itself: colors, firing temperatures, shapes, etc. (Image 12). After we learned some coding and improved the mechanical part of the machine, we could control heavier molds at the desired speed and with enough force. There were many points to work on, and of course, it was not always working the way we wanted (Image 3).

CARLA JOACHIM: We did not have a specific goal in terms of shape and function. Along the process, we tried to constantly question ourselves.

JORDAN MORINEAU: We also looked into different clays: earthenware, porcelain and stoneware. We generated a lot of tests before having consistent results we could reproduce.

ELEONORA D'ASCENZI: What is the role of imperfections in your projects?

JORDAN MORINEAU: The small details and errors are making the object more personal and unique. The "glitch" is what people find the most interesting. Therefore, we are not trying to remove it.

CARLA JOACHIM: The identity of the project "Moca" comes from this contradiction: technology is constant and gives us a sense of control. On the other hand, the use of liquid clay as material is unpredictable. The combination of the two creates imperfection which gives a natural touch.

ELEONORA D'ASCENZI: Since your graduation thesis has been the starting point of your company, what are your suggestions for beginners intended both as students and artisans?

CARLA JOACHIM: Not to be afraid of trying and experimenting. During our graduation, we only had basic knowledge in ceramics and coding, which allowed us to go over the limit of each discipline. It also helps to talk to your colleagues. We had to push each other to discover new things and to question each other.

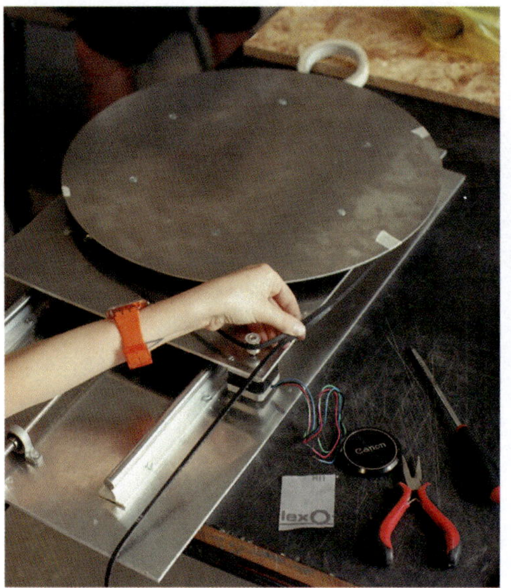

Image 10
©Joachim-Morineau

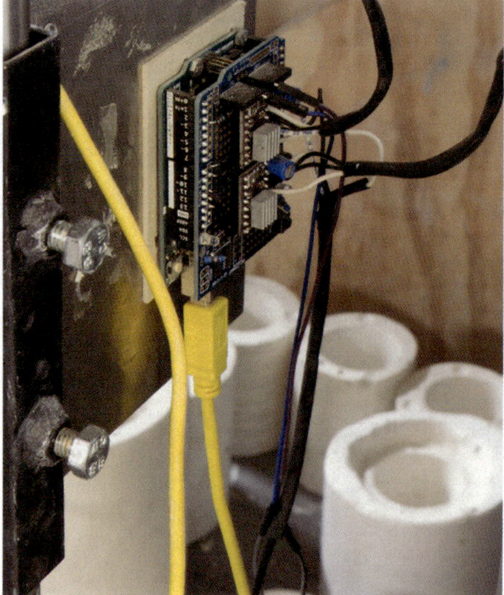

Image 11
©Joachim-Morineau

JORDAN MORINEAU: Our points of view diverge sometimes. We do not see or understand the same things, which can lead to surprising answers.
CARLA JOACHIM: The power of being a student is the environment you are in. It is inspiring and motivating to be surrounded by many different people with different skills and knowledge.
ELEONORA D'ASCENZI: Do you have any future projects taking inspiration from Moca?
JORDAN MORINEAU: There are few projects we did with it. We used the graphic and texture technique to produce different types of tableware for private use and restaurants (Image 13).
CARLA JOACHIM: We are not working on it right now. We are only producing cups (Image 14). In the future, we would like to continue experimenting with the machine. There is a lot to improve.
JORDAN MORINEAU: We believe we should gather more knowledge on the ceramics and the machine/coding part with the help of professionals.

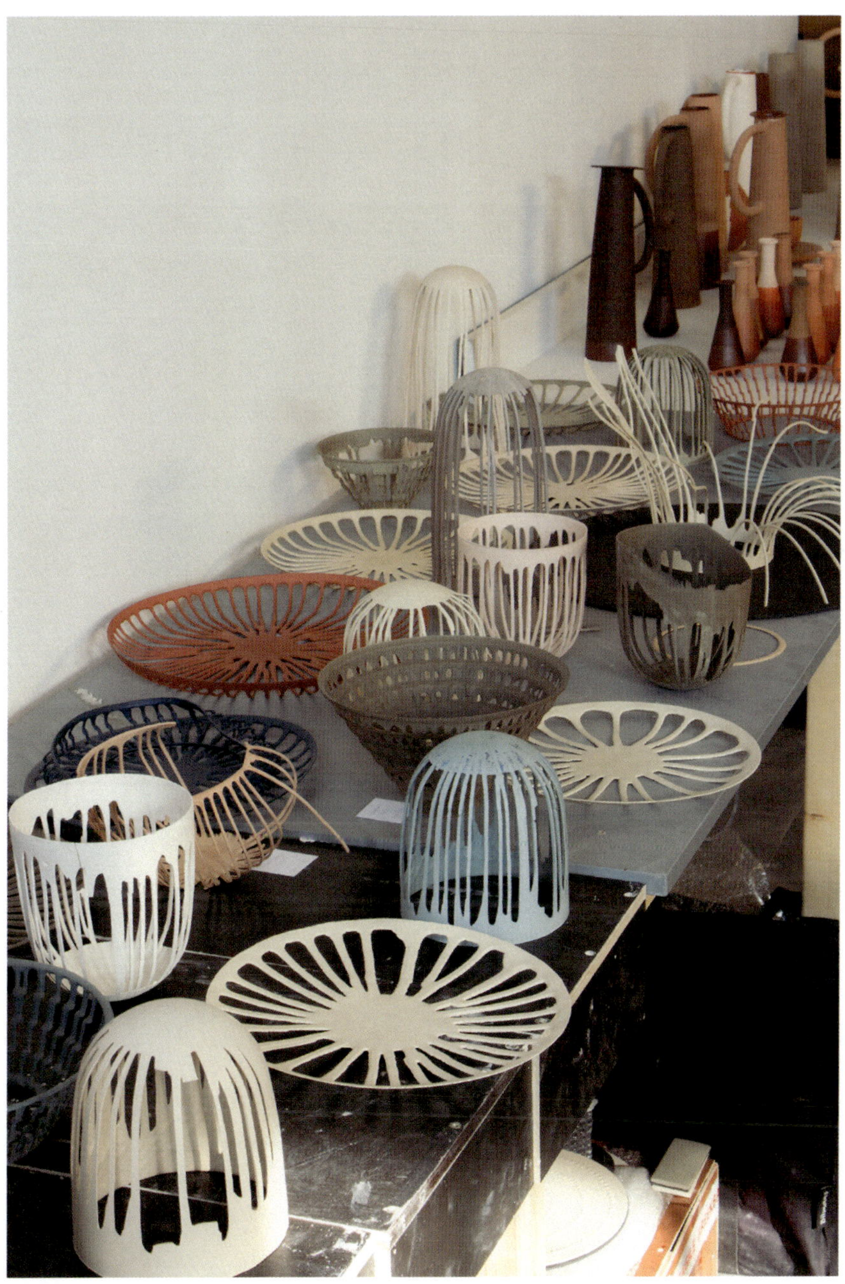

Image 12
©Joachim-Morineau

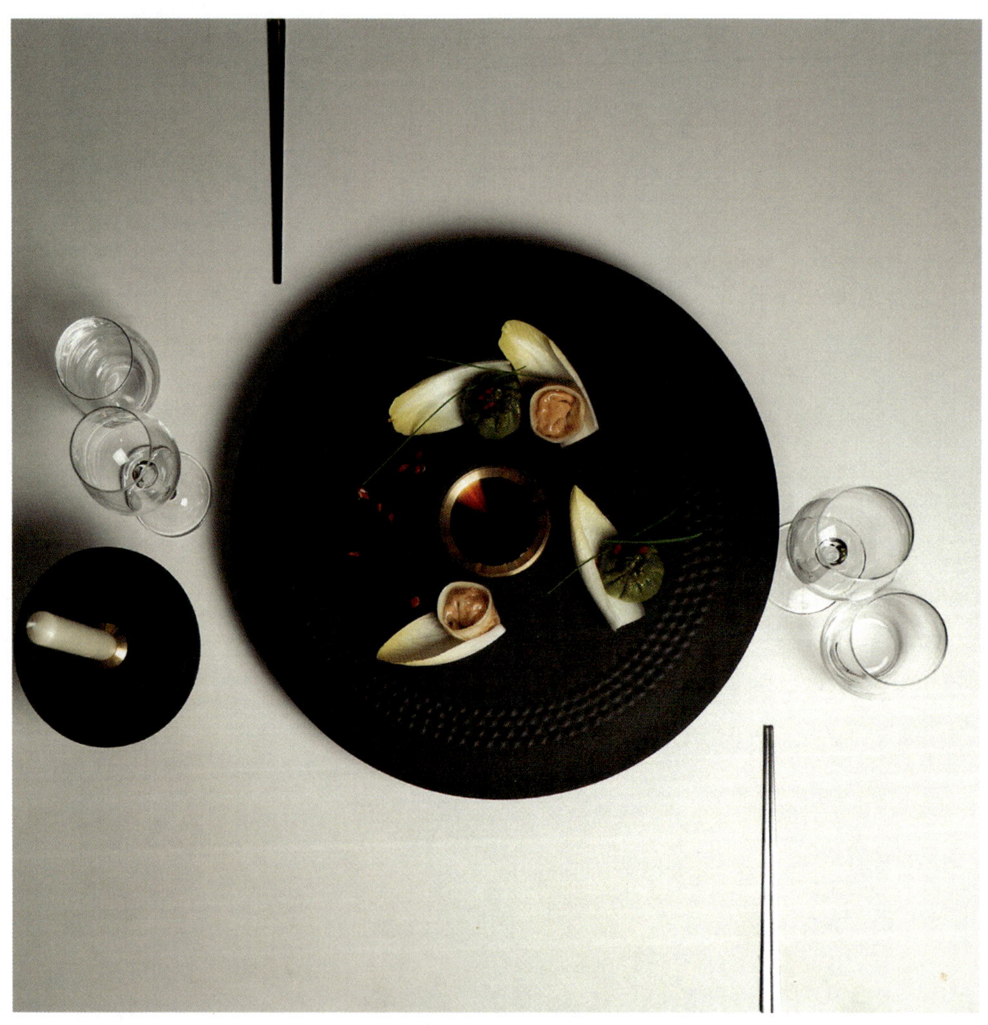

Image 13
©Mikevande Kerkhof

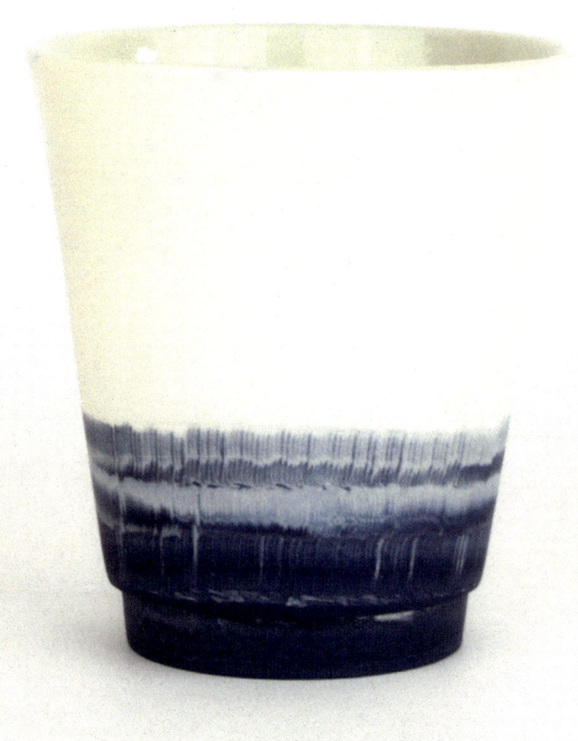

Image 14
©Joachim-Morineau

Andrea Salvatori

Andrea Salvatori was born in 1975 in Faenza (Ra) - Italy; he graduated at the Art Institute for the Ceramic in Faenza in 1995, and he then graduated with a Degree in Sculpture at the Accademia di Belle Arti of Bologna in 2000. During his studies, Andrea learned the secrets of ceramics from the creative duo Bertozzi & Casoni having worked as an apprentice in their studio for many years, in the same way as Renaissance artists learned their practice with the Masters. Since 1997 he has had several individual and collective exhibitions. In 2009 he won the first prize at the 56th edition of the prestigious Premio Faenza, the International Competition Of Contemporary Art Ceramics, for which he ranked second in the prior edition. In 2011 he ranked second at the Sydney Myer Fund Australian Ceramic Award, held at Shepparton Art Museum in Sydney.

ANDREA SALVATORI+ WASP

IKEBANA ROCK'N ROLL

"Ikebana Rock'n Roll" is an innovative project that represents the strength of the integration between digital technologies and handcraft by using Delta WASP 40100 Clay, a 3D printing designed by Wasp as a tool for ceramists. The project outlines new and future artistic scenarios and it is a clear example of how technology could help artisans' work.

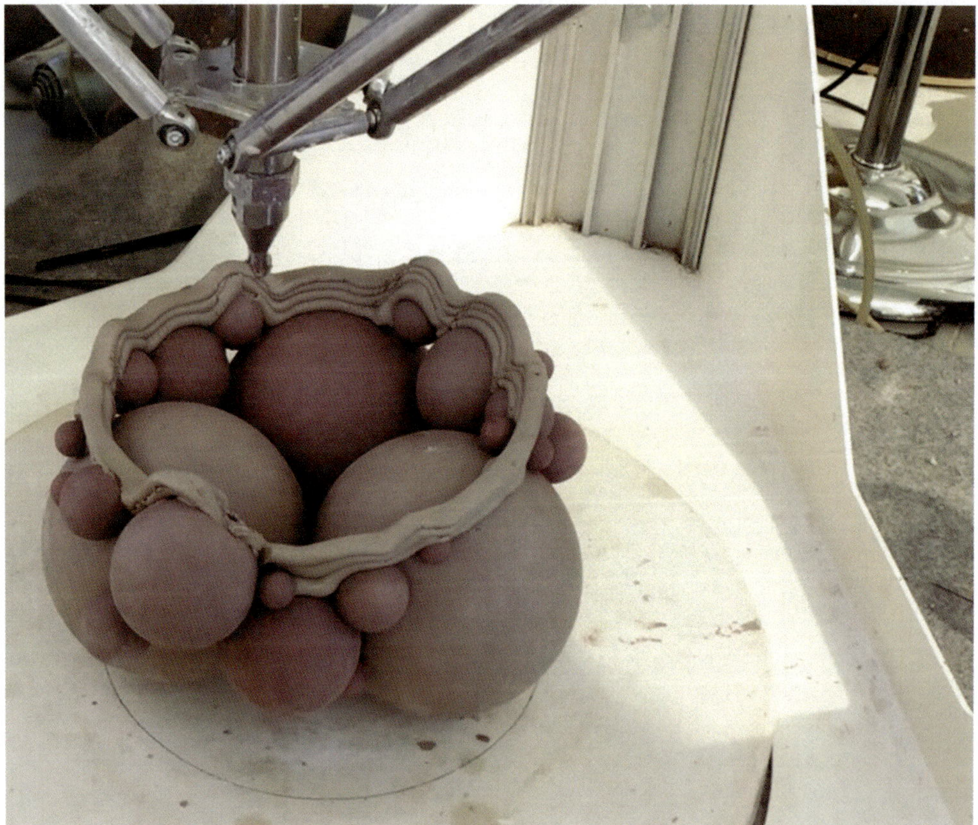

Andrea Salvatori in collaboration with WASP team
©Wasp Team

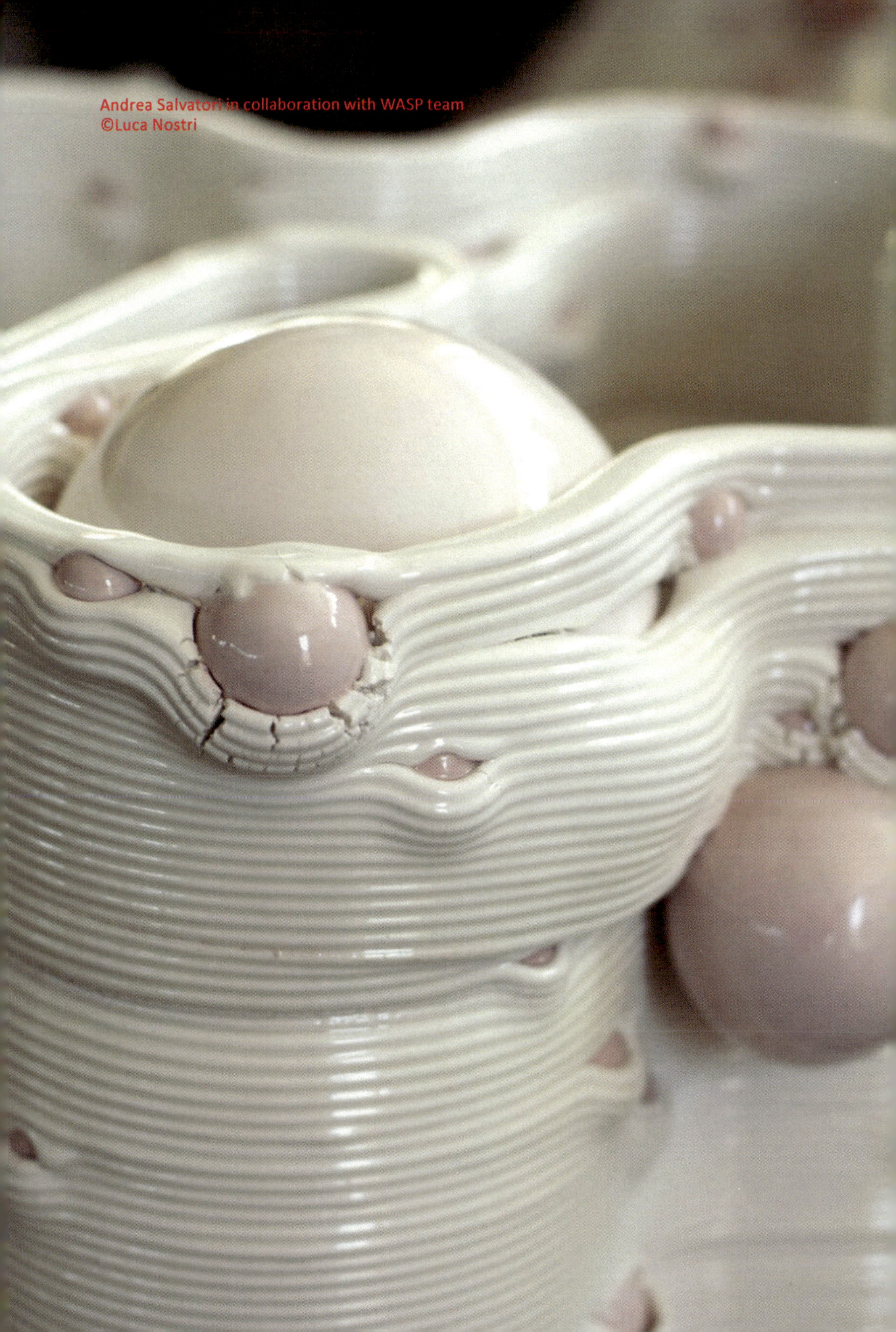

Andrea Salvatori in collaboration with WASP team
©Luca Nostri

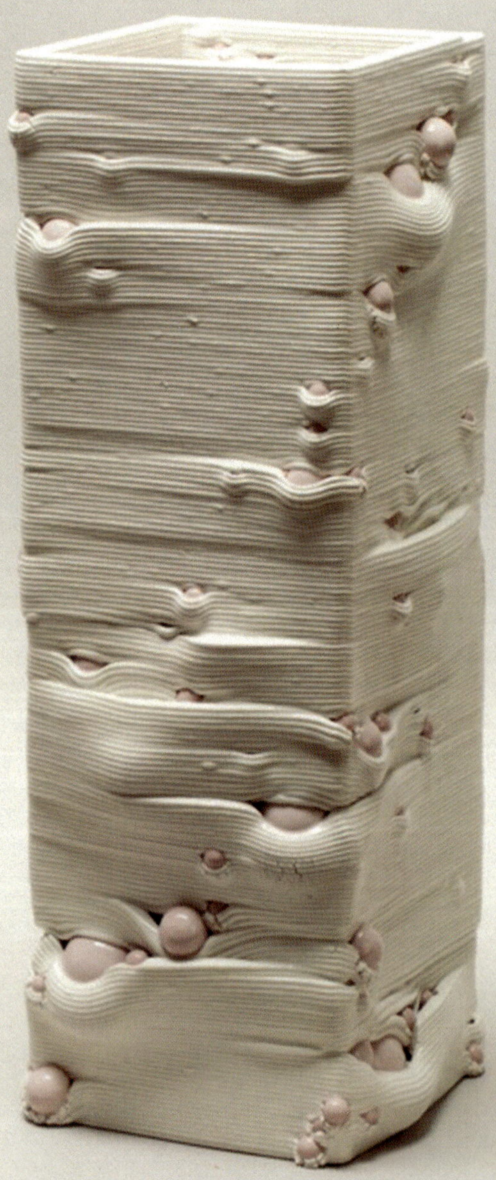

Andrea Salvatori in collaboration with WASP team
©Luca Nostri

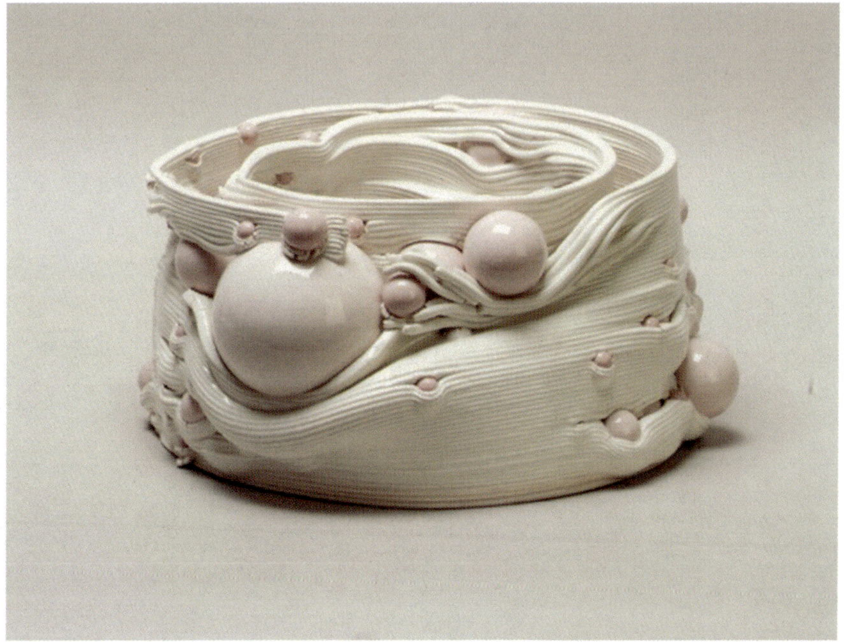

It moreover indicates how the relationship between digital production and handcraft could coexist and bring to a new relationship between human and machinery.
The process sees the handled setting of bubbles by Andrea Salvatori during the 3D ceramic printing. This specific technique applied to non-dried pottery guarantees a unique shape given by the interaction of technology and handcraft.

Text by: Andrea Salvatori

"The design should be centered not only on humans but on the future of the whole biosphere as well.

Paola Antonelli

NATURE

Klarenbeek & Dros

Eric Klarenbeek and Maartje Dros have collaborated on R&D and design projects since 2014, striving for local new economies and production chains, material development and durable design objects. For their projects, they connect universities, high-tech companies as well as farmers with local producers.
The "Mycelium Project" started with the creation of the "Mycelium Chair" (NL, 2010), which was published and exhibited extensively and resulted in the founding of a company for mycelium based products named Krown (NL, 2017). Also the studio worked on the development of biopolymers from local sources, 3D Bakery (NL, 2015), AMS "Circular Supply Chain for the City" (NL, 2016) and the Algae
Lab at Luma, Arles (FR, 2017), resulting in Algae based products by integrating durable and sustainable production methods.
Their newest network is called the Seaweed Circle, integrating and introducing a seaweed based production network focusing on seafarmed biopolymers ©Weedware.

KLARENBEEK & DROS

MYCELIUM CHAIR/THE MYCELIUM PROJECT

Studio Klarenbeek & Dros is the first in the world which has 3D-printed living mycelium, the root structure of mushrooms using this infinite natural source as a living glue for binding organic waste.
They started with the "Mycelium Chair" as the archetype for a functional design object.

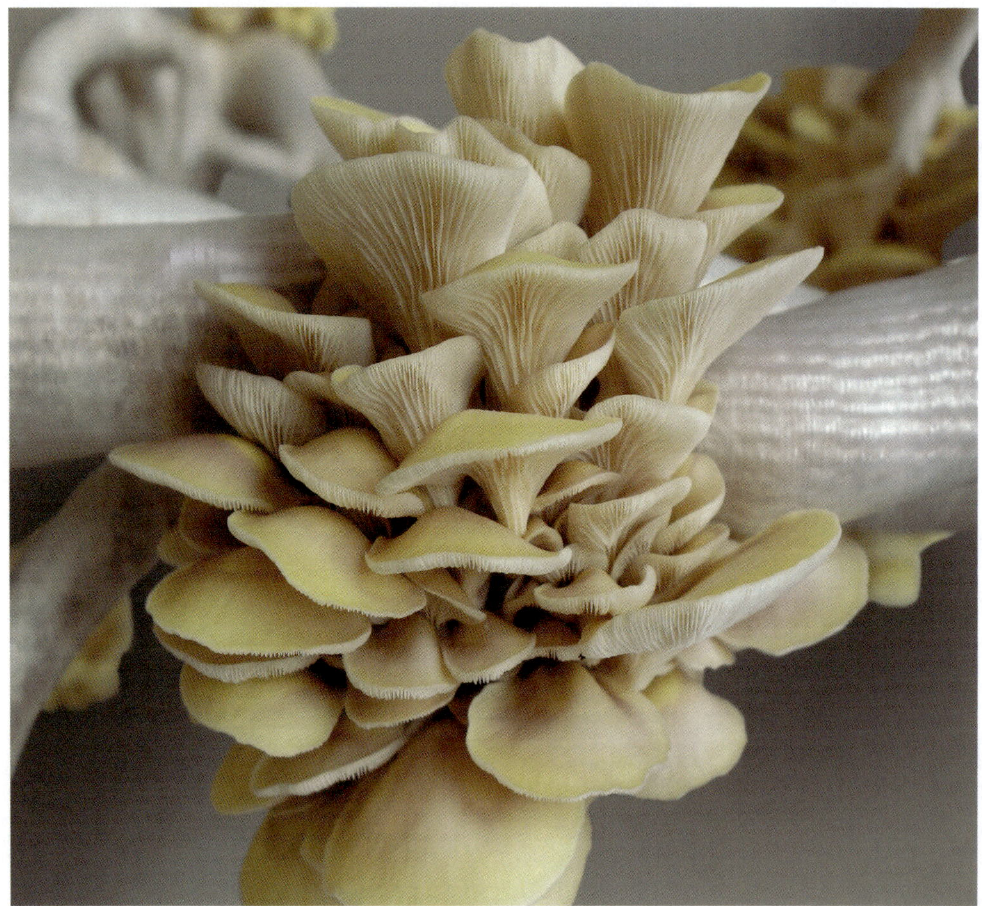

©Studio Klarenbeek & Dros

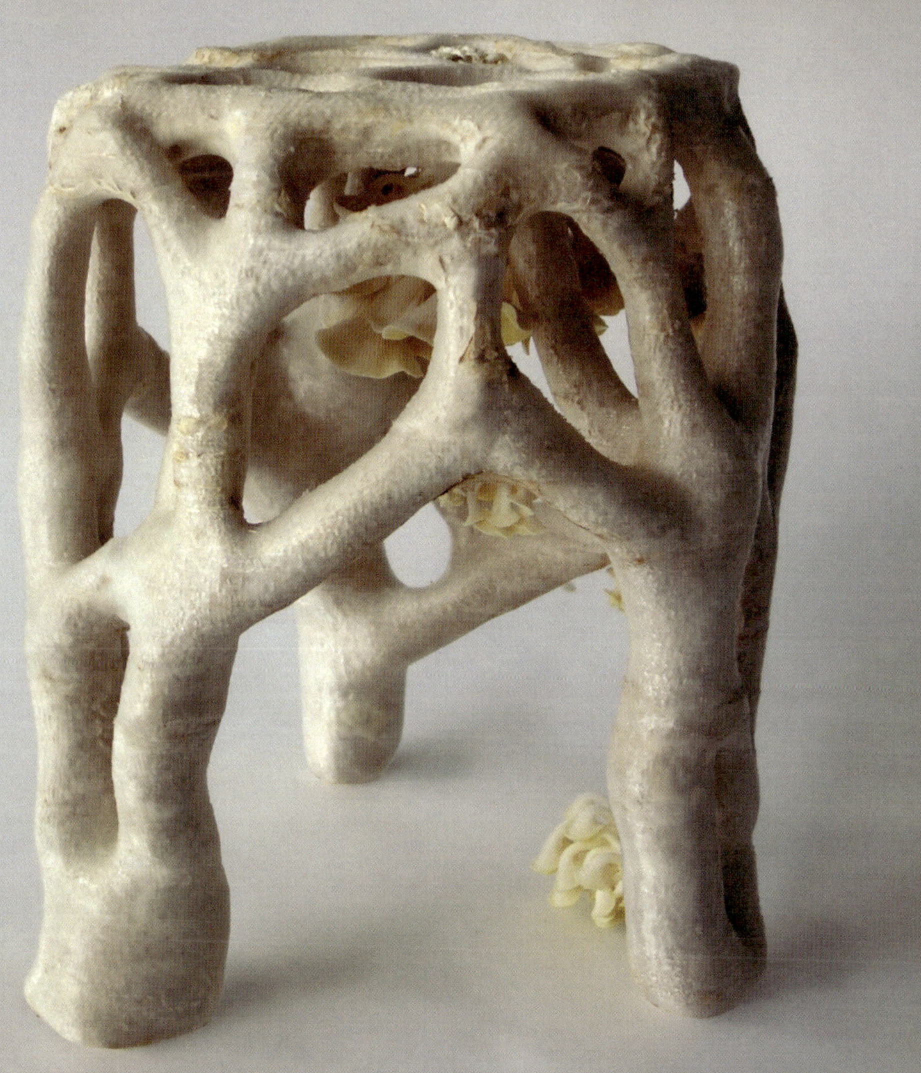

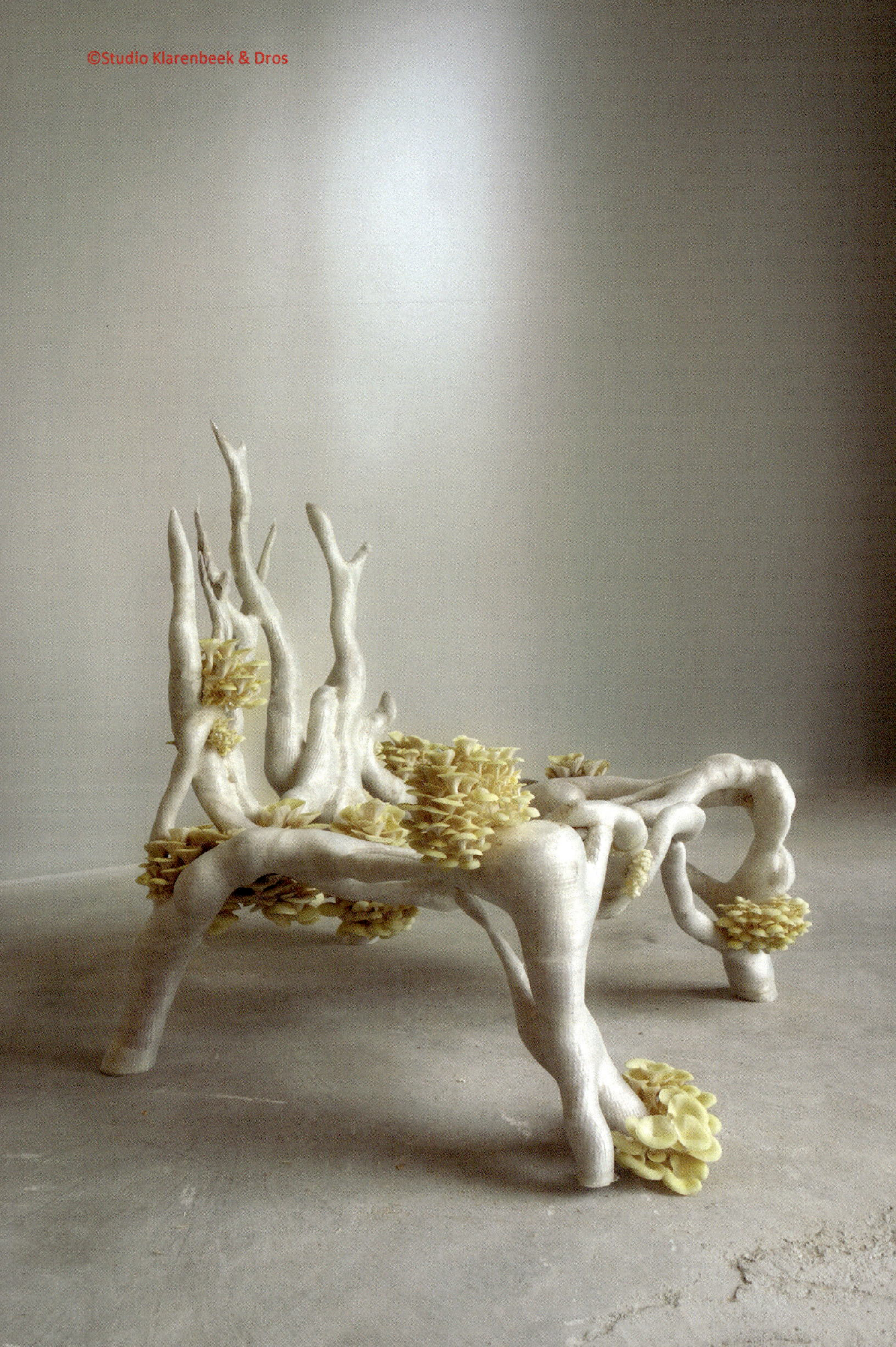
©Studio Klarenbeek & Dros

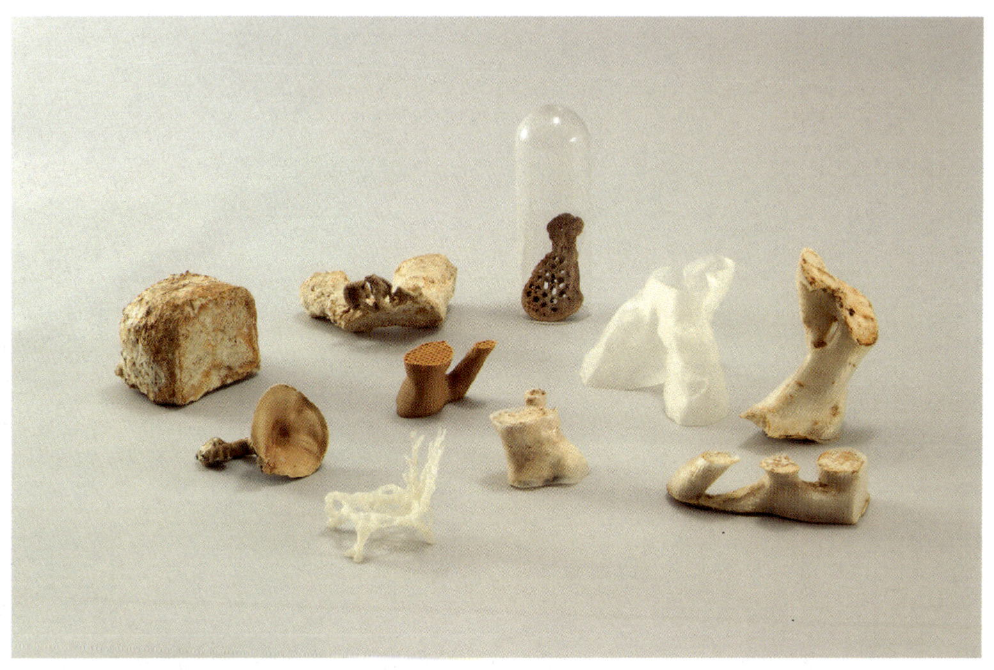

The chair is inspired by mycelial networks and reflects the unimaginable freedom of 3D printing. Another project, "Veiled Lady", Mycelium Project 2.0, is printed in one go and inspired by the net structure of its equally named fungus: Veiled Lady.
After its use, the product is fully compostable and can be disposed of without harming the environment. On the contrary, it will fertilize our surroundings!

Text by: Studio Klarenbeek & Dros

Studio Swine

Studio Swine (Super Wide Interdisciplinary New Explorers) is a group established in 2011 by Azusa Murakami (JP) and Alexander Groves (UK).
Their work straddles between the spheres of sculpture, installations and cinema, blending poetry and research into immersive experiences. The studio adopts an unique approach to each work, drawing on the distinctive resources and vernacular aesthetics of its cultural, historic and economic landscape. Studio Swine's films have been awarded at Cannes and other film festivals around the world and their work have been widely exhibited at institutions such as the V&A Museum in London, Venice Art and Architecture Biennale. Their works have been collected by MoMA New York and Centre Pompidou in Paris.

STUDIO SWINE

GYRECRAFT

"Gyrecraft" is a new project by Studio Swine, in which they have transformed plastic pollution found at the sea into a collection of luxury objects. It was the focus of an expedition across the North Atlantic Ocean, undertaken by Studio Swine co-founders, Alexander Groves and Azusa Murakami in the autumn of 2014.

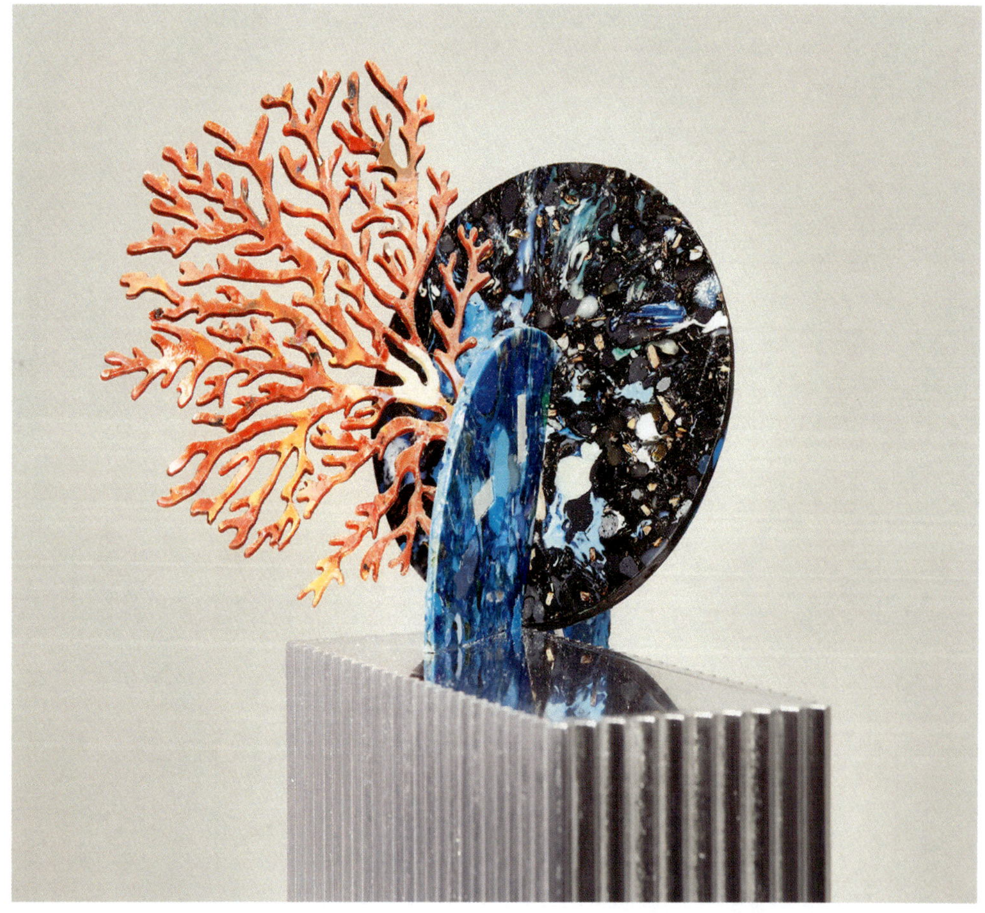

©Petr Krejčí

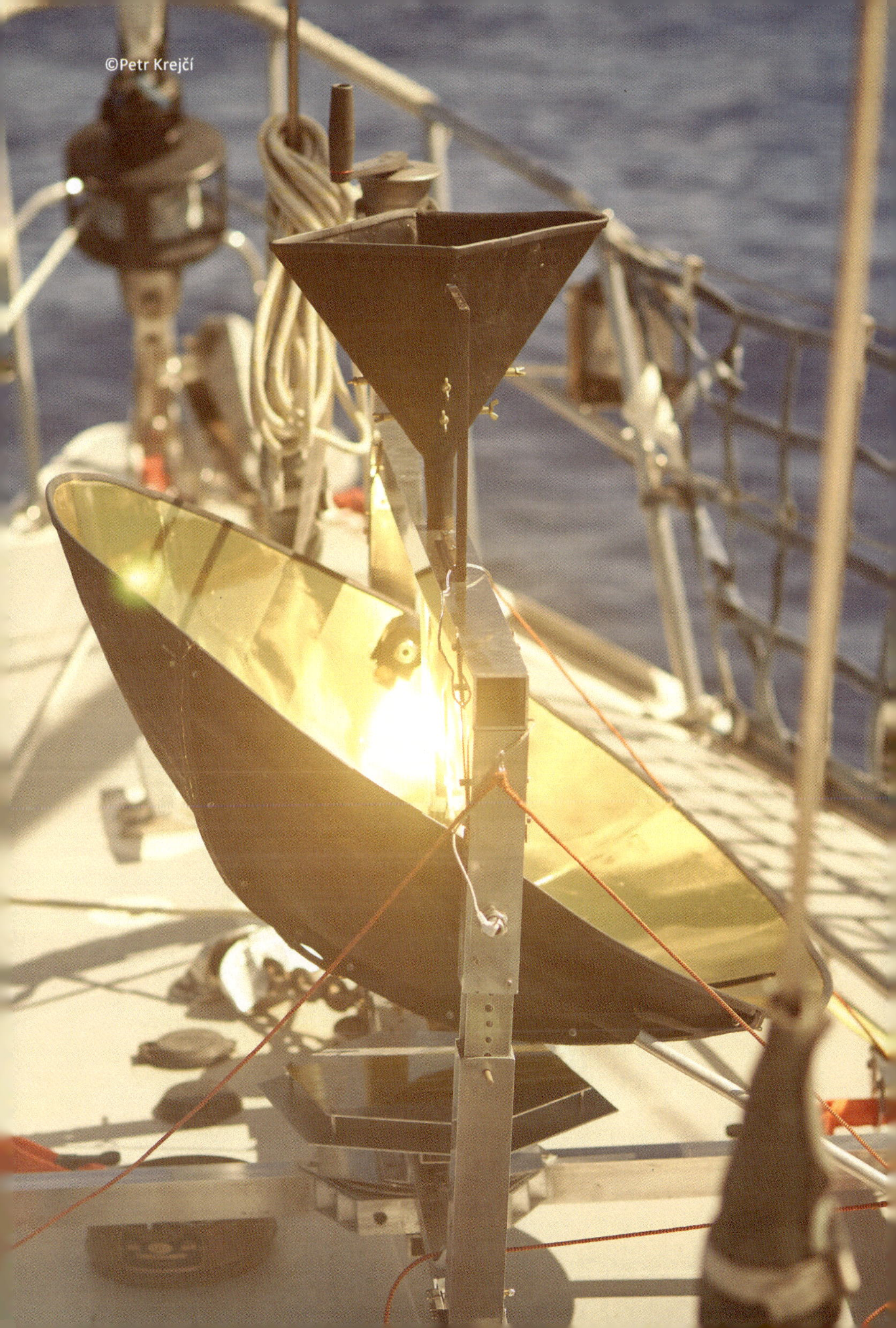
©Petr Krejčí

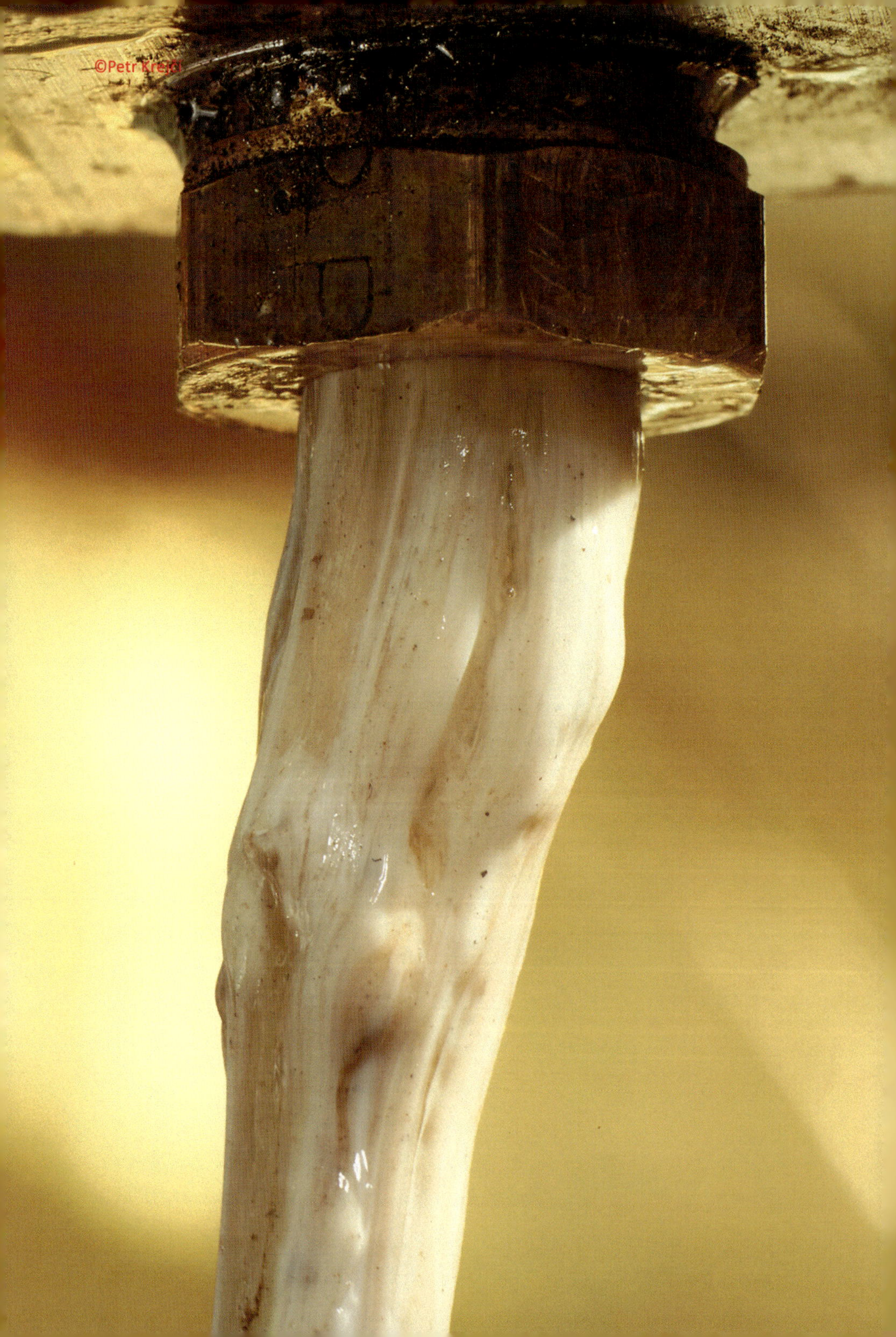
©Petr Krejčí

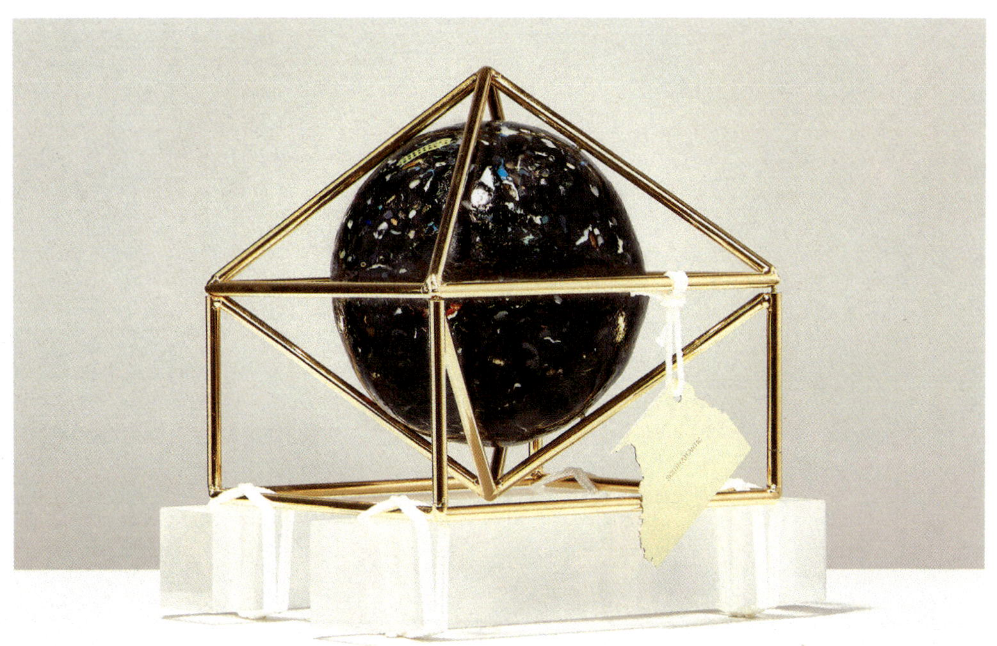

In order to transform this plastic flotsam and jetsam into new works, they invented and built their own Solar Extruder, which melts and extrudes sea plastic using sunlight.
Traditionally, many of these crafts took place onboard during long voyages as a way of making vital repairs or simply passing the time at sea.
"Gyrecraft" is the intersection of the dwindling and under-valued heritage of local maritime crafts and the rapid rise of sea plastic pollution.

Text by: Studio Swine

"Cultural heritage as the legacy of physical artifacts and intangible attributes of a group or society.

UNESCO

craft 4.0 for
CULTURE

Tomáš Gabzdil Libertíny

Currently living and working in Rotterdam, Tomáš Libertíny was born in Slovakia and he studied at the Technical University Košice in Slovakia focusing on engineering and design. He was awarded George Soros's Open Society Institute Scholarship to study at The University of Washington in Seattle, where he focused on painting and sculpture. He continued his study at the Academy of Fine Arts and Design in Bratislava in painting and conceptual design. After receiving the prestigious Huygens Scholarship, he enrolled in the Master's program at the Design Academy Eindhoven where he received his MFA in 2006. Tomáš Libertíny's fascination with the beauty and intelligence of nature fuels his work with timeless yet relatable emotions. The relationship between Man and Nature, both psychological and physical, serves as a constant source of inspiration.

TOMÁŠ LIBERTÍNY

ETERNITY (A.K.A. NEFERTITY)/ HONEYCOMB AMPHORA

The monumental "Eternity" was made in collaboration with 60.000 honeybees, invited by the artist to build their beeswax honeycombs around the skeleton of the Bust of Nefertiti. The bust is based on the 3D model of the original portrait of the Egyptian queen. The long process had two stages.

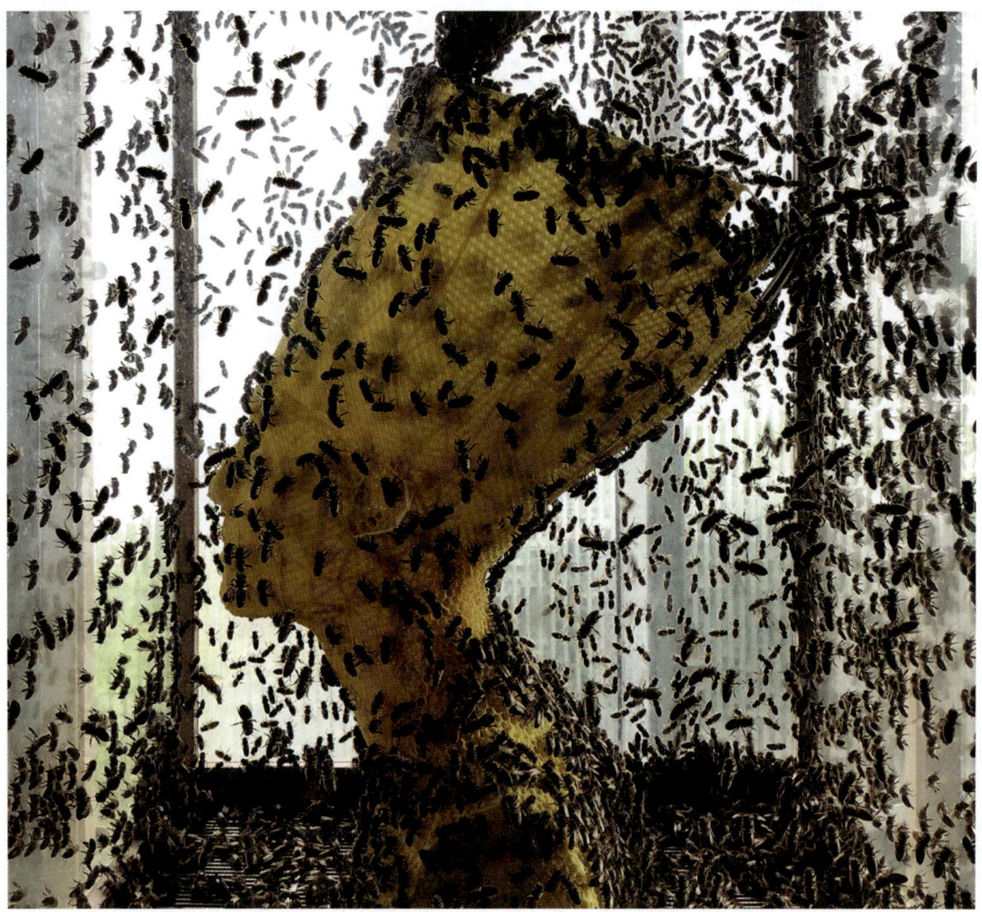

©Titia Hahne

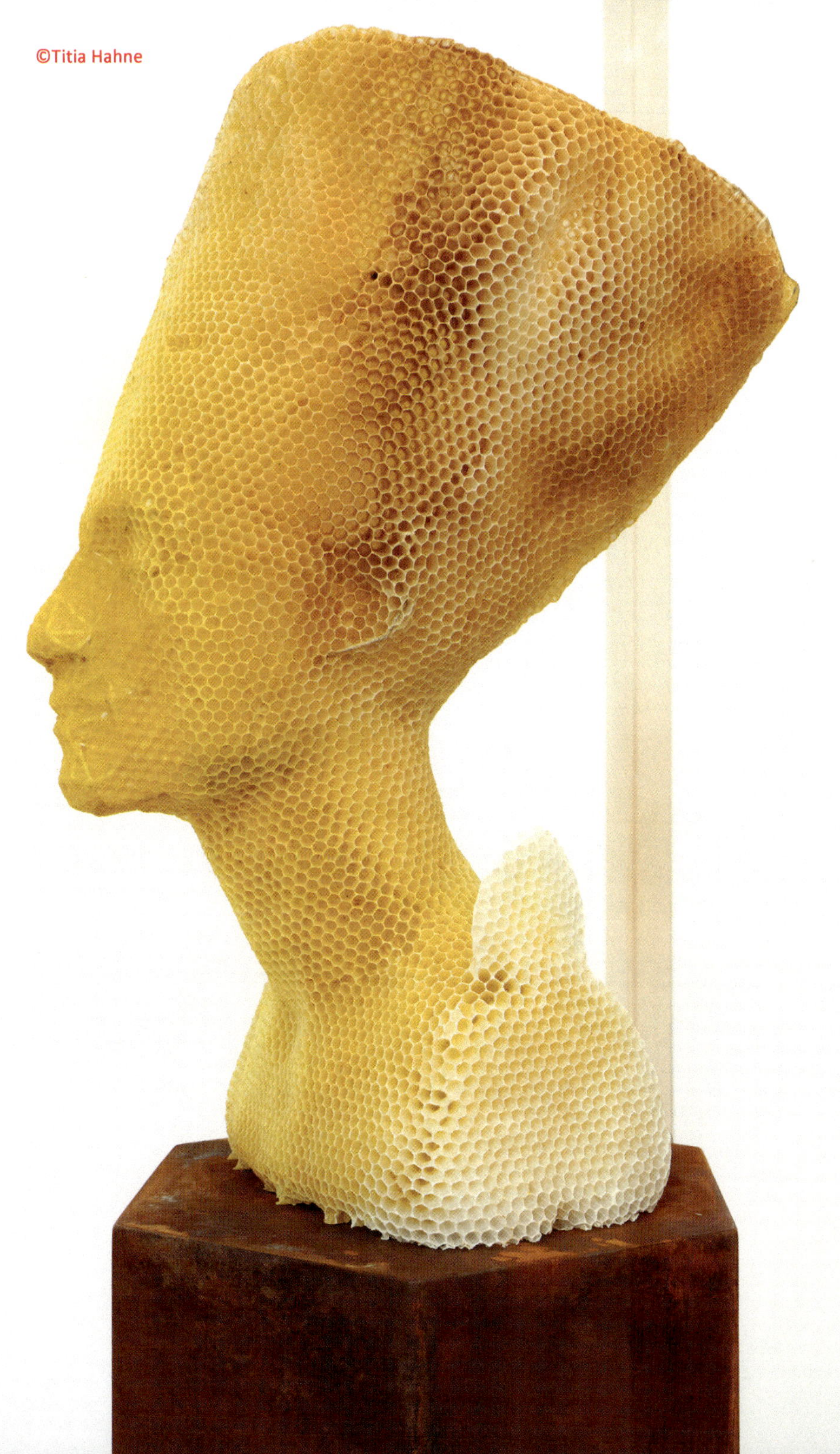
©Titia Hahne

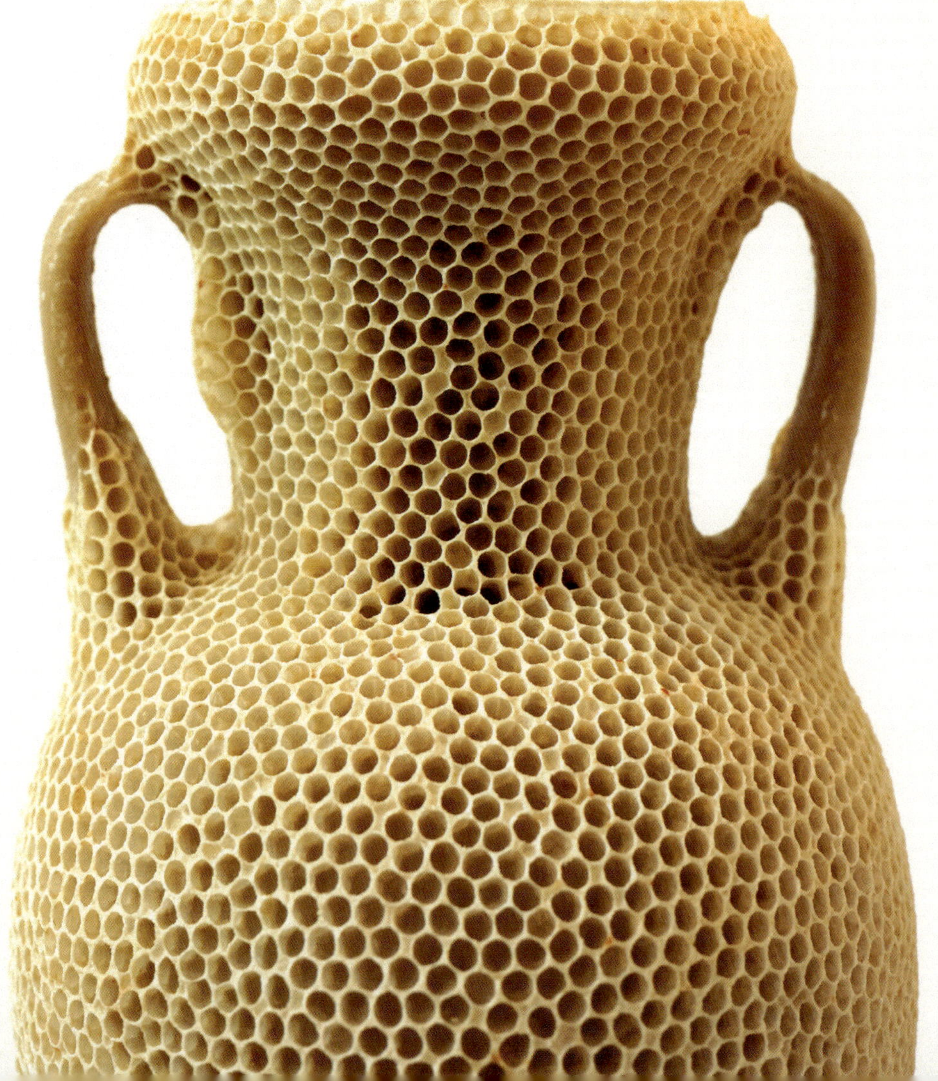

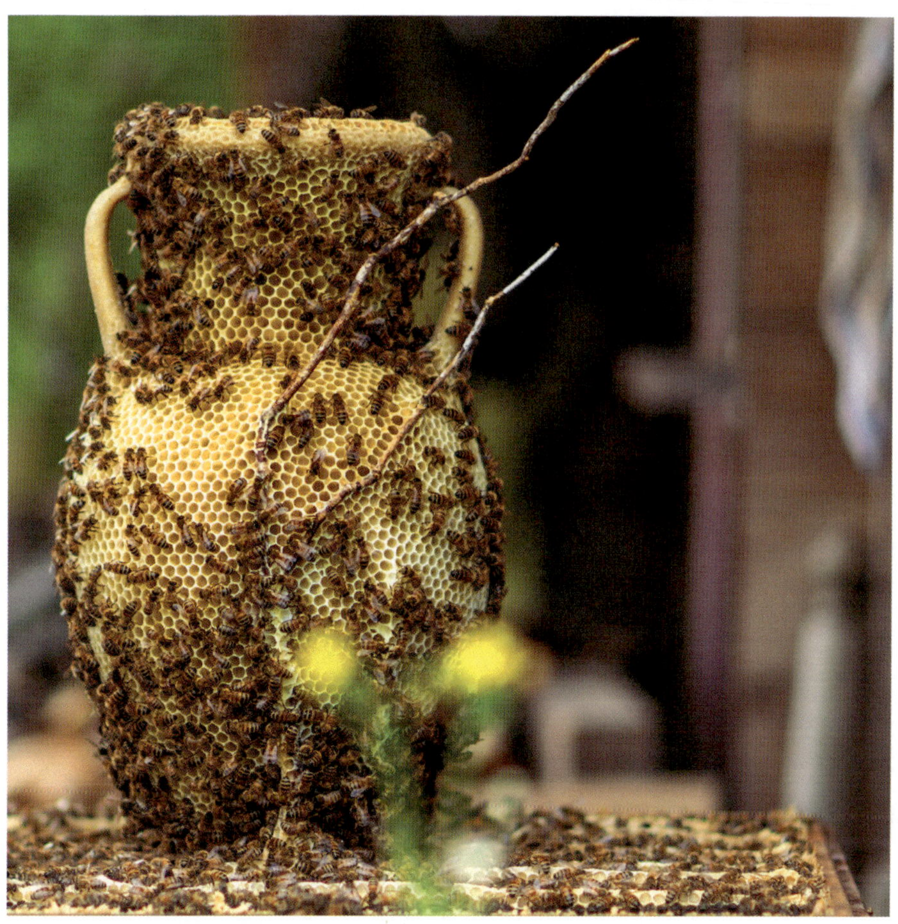

©Titia Hahne

The first one when it was shown at Kunsthal in Rotterdam in the summer of 2019 as a live installation where visitors had the chance to observe the process of bees building the artwork at the museum. The second one when it was completely finished in 2020 and exhibited as part of Tomáš Libertíny's solo show "Melancholia" at Rademakers Gallery in Amsterdam. Honeycomb represents an ancient Greek amphora and it is completely made by bees, based on the famous Nolan amphora type from the Metropolitan Museum of Art.

Text by: Tomáš Libertíny

TALK-live transcript

ELEONORA D'ASCENZI: Now we can move on to the next speaker, Tomáš Libertíny. Tomáš was born in Slovakia and now he is currently living in Rotterdam where he's exploring the relationship between man and nature. His project is part of the culture section since the "Nefertiti" project and the Honeycomb Amphora could represent the use of craft 4.0 for cultural heritage dissemination. I just want to bring to light one curiosity about this project: he collaborated with 60.000 bees for the "Nefertiti" project. So, Tomáš, thank you for being here today. Please tell us more about your projects and your concept ideas.

TOMÁŠ GABZDIL LIBERTÍNY: Thank you Eleonora for the nice introduction and hello everyone. Congratulations to all the designers who have presented the projects, I love them all. They are really beautiful and inspiring. I have prepared the presentation only dedicated to the two projects that we are exhibiting.

The first is the "Honeycomb Amphora" and, as the title suggests, this has been made by bees.

I started working with the bees quite a long time ago. Nature serves me all the time not only as an inspiration, but also as a way of falling in love with the organism of bees and their colony in order to investigate the materials that come from the beehive, which is the beeswax itself.

I started with beeswax and this was typical of classical sculptors who created shapes and objects molding and shaping them with the tools they have at their disposal. However, I wanted to push the project a little bit further at that time. For this reason, I thought it would be an interesting thing to directly go to the source and invite bees to build the object directly from the beeswax instead of being made by the artist as the bricklayer makes the house for himself, using the clay from the mountain and nature forces himself to create the house.

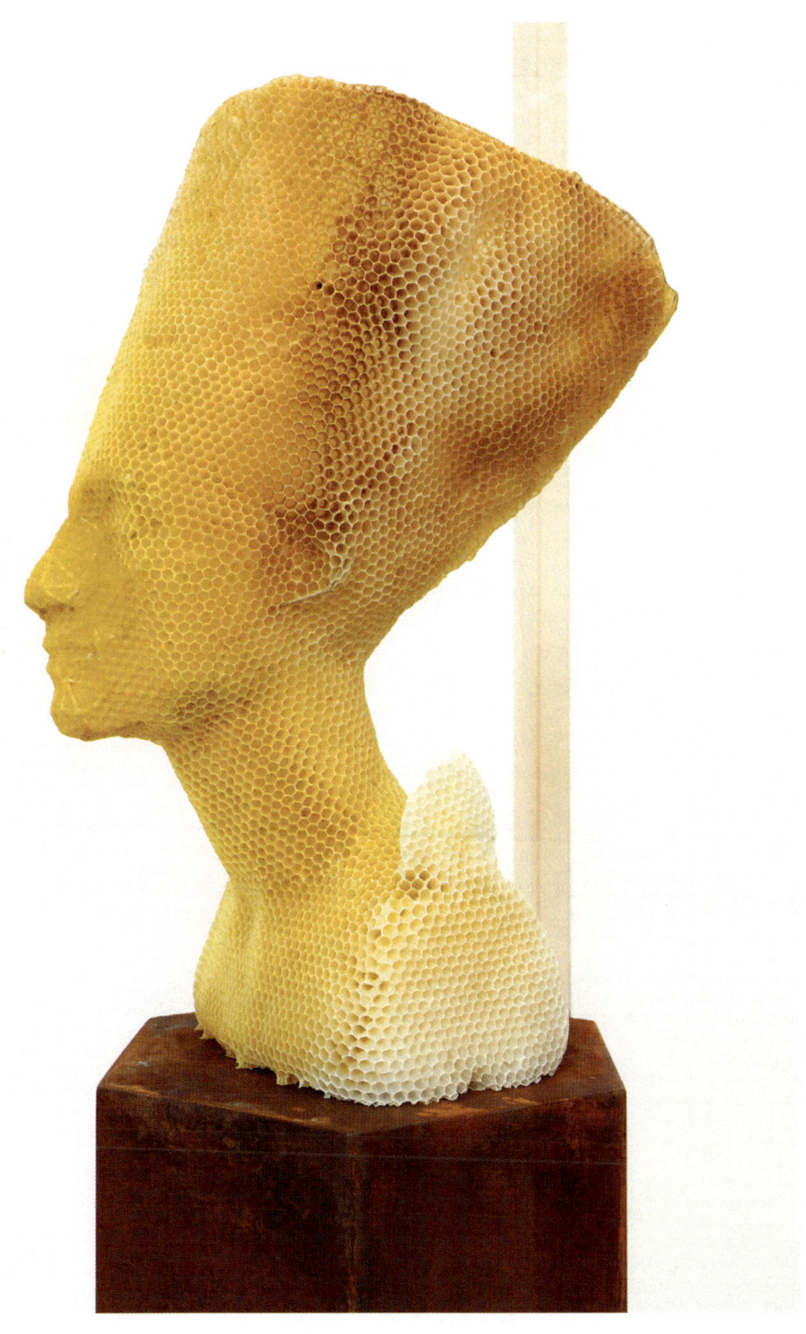

Image 1
©Titia Hahne

I took inspiration from the difference between the Roman and the Greek amphitheater. Usually, the ancient Greek amphitheaters are built-in landscapes using the territory around to support the architecture whereas on the contrary, for example, the Roman ones, which were much more advanced in technology, did not need that support of nature. They could sustain it with their technical genius. And a great example is the Colosseum in the center of Rome, which is a cell standing structure. Greeks, instead, would have built that inside the mountain using the shape of the valleys and the hills.

So, the project started investigating how bees work and what kind of shapes they build. I found out that they are very likely to respond to these kinds of pregnant shapes, very much connected with the vases.

And it was also the matter of trying to combine concave and convex shapes to create more experimentation not only in terms of shapes, but also in terms of color. So, we found a way to invite the bees to change the color. And there is an example of a red amphora. A bit of a curiosity: bees don't see red color and they usually pollinate white flowers, about 45% of all the flowers in the world are white. The reason is that white reflects most UV light. So next time you see a white flower, you can be sure that it is very much appealing for bees.

For the project that I'm displaying (Image 1) I don't use any kind of artificial skeleton, but just the beeswax itself of an already existing shape - that comes from the "Nolan amphora" of the Metropolitan Museum of Art in New York. This is usually used for storing a very dense liquid that we know now as wine. So, there is a relationship between the shape and the material itself.

And then the sculpture that you mentioned: the Nefertiti. It is officially called "Eternity" because as in the "Honeycomb Amphora", the Nefertiti is only part of the sculpture. And the inspiration comes from Pygmalion, the well-known myth of the king and his sculptor who created the white marble piece of Pygmalion that became alive and from which a love story started.

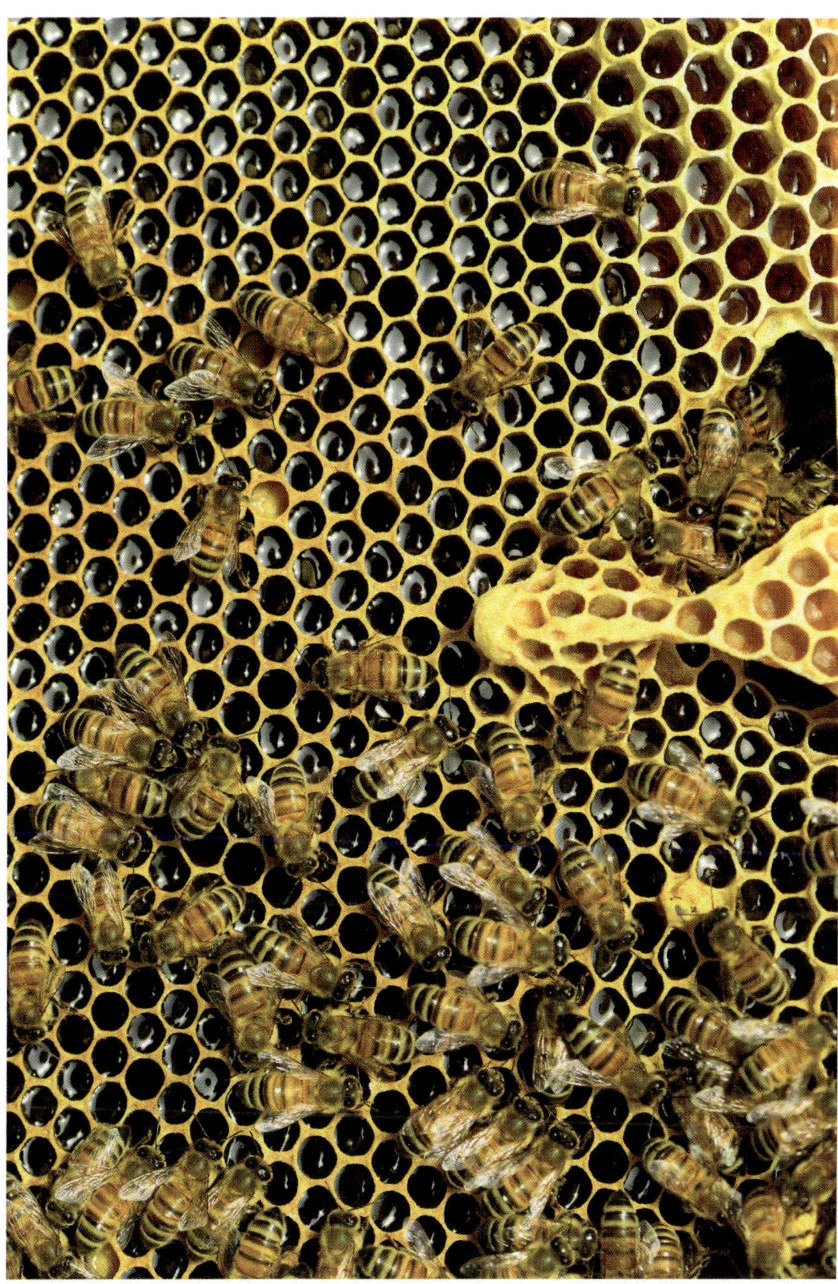

Beehive detail

I fell in love with Nefertiti and I wanted to bring her alive (Image 2). She has a beautiful story: around 1920 she was discovered by Ludwig Borchardt and brought to Germany. Now she is in the Neues Museum. The story is very interesting because Nefertiti was the wife of the pharaoh, the queen. And interestingly, her husband, Pharaoh Akhenaten, started as one of the first pioneers of monotheistic religion. He broke away from polytheism, established by the history of Egypt, but ran by a multitude of priests. And he abandoned that vision of starting a new city. His only God was Athen, son of God. And interestingly enough, the temples that they used for celebration had opened roofs to let the sun get inside the temples. They were open-air for celebrating nature herself without closing it off with architecture. I find it really interesting. Nevertheless, this experiment didn't last very long: after the death of Akhenaten, the religion was abandoned. And I think that is why we do not know much about the details of Nefertiti's or Akhenaten's lives: because of this rejection to their monotheism.

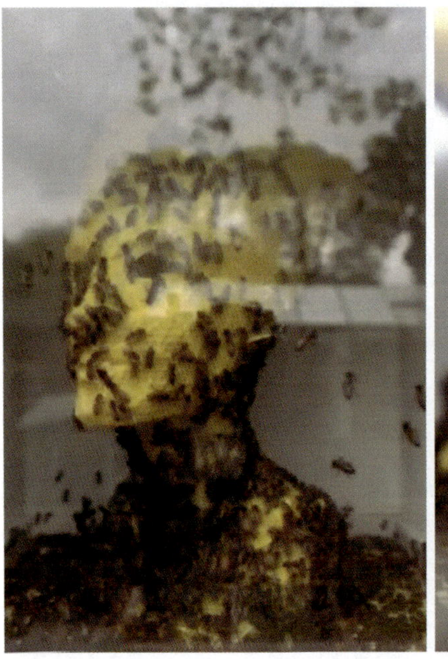
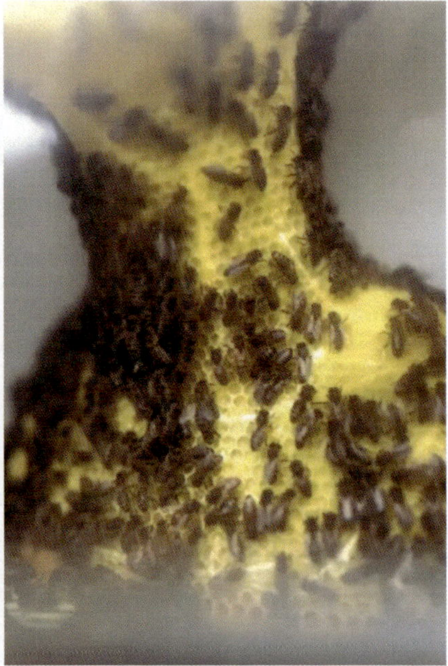

Image 2
©Tomáš Libertíny

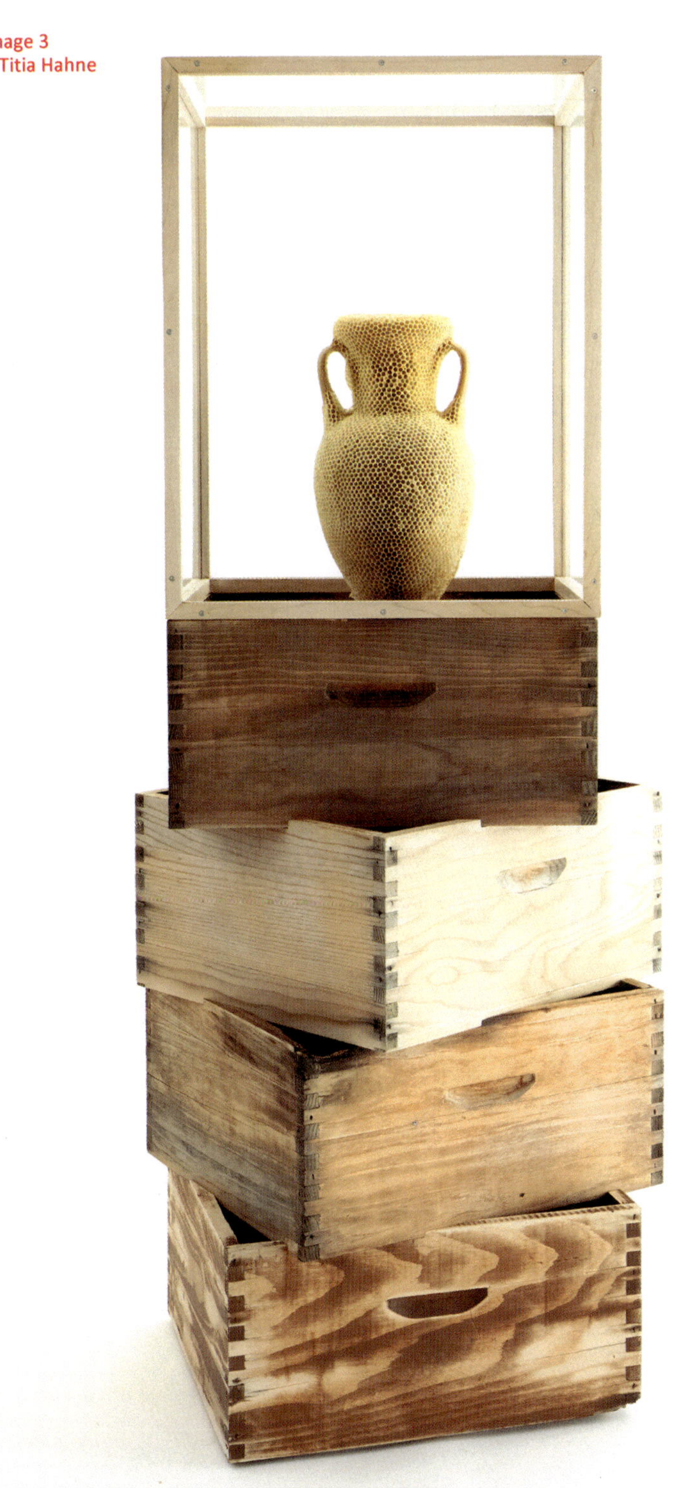

It's an interesting story because there was not a purely digital model available to be used. We made a 3D model and we 3D printed the skeleton that was suitable for the bees to build around. We've done this before, so I knew what I was doing. It was not so much of an experiment, but more stretching on how far we could go with this technique that we developed (Image 3). And so, we prepared this whole installation almost to be resembling the situation in Berlin. I do not know if any of you have been there, but there is a kind of single room dedicated to Nefertiti. She is in the glass cabinet, on the pedestal. And this was the same situation in the beehive. For the process itself I invited 60.000 bees, as Eleonora rightly pointed out.

They worked on it for two years: we started in 2019 and we finished in 2020. It took a very long time. So, this is a short video (Image 4) from the process itself: beautiful to see, but also quite phobic if you have something against insects. There is something beautiful and repulsive at the same time in this image. But I like the contrast between the natural skin built by the bees and the little bit of the protrusion of the 3D printed skeleton that almost resembles the bone structure. Wex is, by its nature, a very healing material, since it contains propolis. So there is something fascinating about using that as a skin.

So, this (Image 1) is the final sculpture of Nefertiti that became alive like in the story of Pygmalion. And it is part of the installation of the curtain-steel pedestal on which she sits. This is also a natural process
in terms of how iron ages and oxidizes protecting itself and then locks itself from further deterioration. So rust is also natural protection towards longevity. So thank you very much for the attention and I give the floor back to you Eleonora.

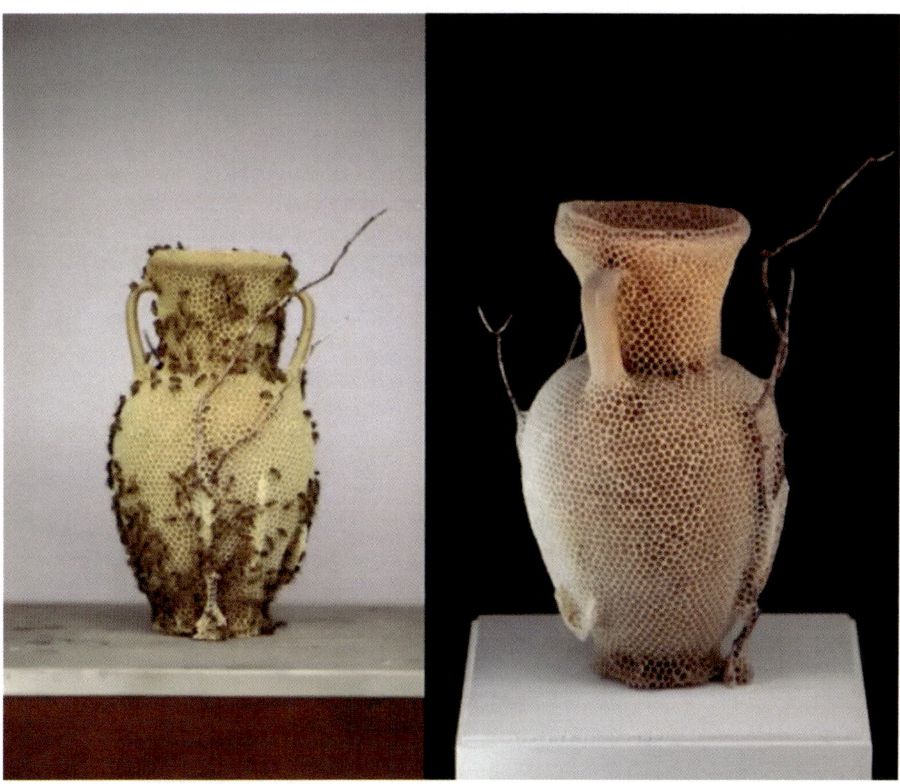

Image 4
©Tomáš Libertíny

ELEONORA D'ASCENZI: Thank you Tomaš, really thank you for your presentation, for your interesting pictures as well as the historical background. I think that your presence, as well as the other projects, definitely represents how we can "think out of the box".

ELEONORA D'ASCENZI: I have some questions for you, Tomaš. What was the realization timing for "Nefertiti" and the "Honeycomb Amphora"?
TOMÁŠ GABZDIL LIBERTÍNY: Two years for the "Nefertiti" and one season for the "Honeycomb Amphora". But this is how bees usually work in nature. They are most active in terms of building honeycombs and producing wax between April and June. You have this window of about three months every year that you can make sure that they have a lot of activity and then they will produce something extra so you do not exploit them later in the season when they need it for themselves. So, if somehow you missed that in summertime, you would not succeed. You have to wait for another half a year. So that is why it takes two years, because actually if you do not do it in a couple of months, you have to wait for another year.
ELEONORA D'ASCENZI: Is there a kind of "slow-life" chosen process?
TOMÁŠ GABZDIL LIBERTÍNY: So, I think I got into it because I am by nature anxious and fast, and this process compensates a lot of that. So, you calm down doing this and it teaches you a lot. I mean, it is an incredibly slow process. And one thing that I learned is that you have very little control. My father is an architect and I studied at the Design Academy and in various schools, as well as designers, architects, and I would say we are accustomed to have plans, have things under control, and anticipate the outcome to predict things. This kind of natural based-design process teaches you a lot of humbleness, patience and reflection, and if you are the type of personality that is looking for fast results trying hard to get what you want, this can be a problem. So, I think I choose it consciously to work with nature because it comes down to the aspect of my character. So it's a really beautiful thing to work with bees.
ELEONORA D'ASCENZI: So, it was a personal need to adopt a slow life process. There is another question for you. What do you think about the relationship between people, nature and technology? Could design and craftsmanship play a crucial role?

TOMÁŠ GABZDIL LIBERTÍNY: Well, Tim already mentioned a little bit about it: it is so complicated. I mean, on the one hand, you have sustainability, global warming, impact of our lives on a major planet and on the other hand you have technology and speed advancing incessantly. And then we get anxiety from not being able to keep up with it. That means a generational problem. People, who were born a decade ago, have got accustomed to it, it is old news. And this was a kind of a historical shift because when you were born in the nineteen hundreds, the world was about the same until the Industrial Revolution, nothing changed. So would you be used to gradually, very slowly changing. We will not be able to rely on the steadiness and something that is forever to stay, this flexibility of mind and our brains being organic as they are, we'll have to adapt much faster than in the past. And I think, of course, it will change biologically because there is this beautiful relationship between culture and nurturing. So, I mean, we have the predisposition to react and adapt. That is also why we are on top of this food chain and we are the species controlling the planet because we can adapt the most and react to the environmental changes.

But, on the other hand, I love technology and I am always amazed where and how far it goes. But I do not always think progress is good. And the dichotomy of the relationship between technology and progress is beautiful. Progress is inevitable, but progress does not guarantee that everything will always go for the best. Progress and change will come and this is for sure. So what? What I think is more interesting to look at - and maybe more vital - is the metaphysical point of view values and what matters. Because we have a technology that is becoming a religion and science becomes religion by itself. But now the options are almost endless. It becomes a question of choice. I mean, in that situation, you need to have quite a big moral and ethical compass on what you are choosing to do, what is the right thing to do. So, I think there will be a little bit of a return to forms of morality and the return of mainstream philosophies. It is a kind of beautiful mixture of them both. And you already see it in a lot of mainstream and popular philosophers who are serving us as sort of everyday gurus on "how to live life well", a sort of this Michel de Montaigne's idea.

Kourosh Asgar-Irani

Kourosh is an Architect and designer who grew up in Vienna after his parents left Iran during the Iran - Iraq war. As a child, he used the structure of the Persian rugs that adorned his family home to create a road network for his matchbox cars. Studying architecture in Vienna and Los Angeles, he learned his skills from Zaha Hadid, who was his professor at the University of Applied Arts in Vienna. When he started collecting antique rugs, he developed an interest in the appearance of carpet motifs reminiscent of the aesthetics of 8-bit gaming systems.
He identified an opportunity to apply the parametric software tools he was using in his practice to create bespoke patterns and started "Rugture".
He is now based between London and Vienna and also sees "Rugture" as an opportunity to reconnect with his Persian roots.

KOUROSH ASGAR-IRANI

RUGTURE

"Rugture" is a modern interpretation of classic oriental rugs, which are conceived using generative design methods and then traditionally hand-knotted in Tabriz, Persia. Using architectural parametric 3D-software, the patterns are based on traditional nomadic designs from Persia, Anatolia, Armenia, Central Asia, and southern Russia.

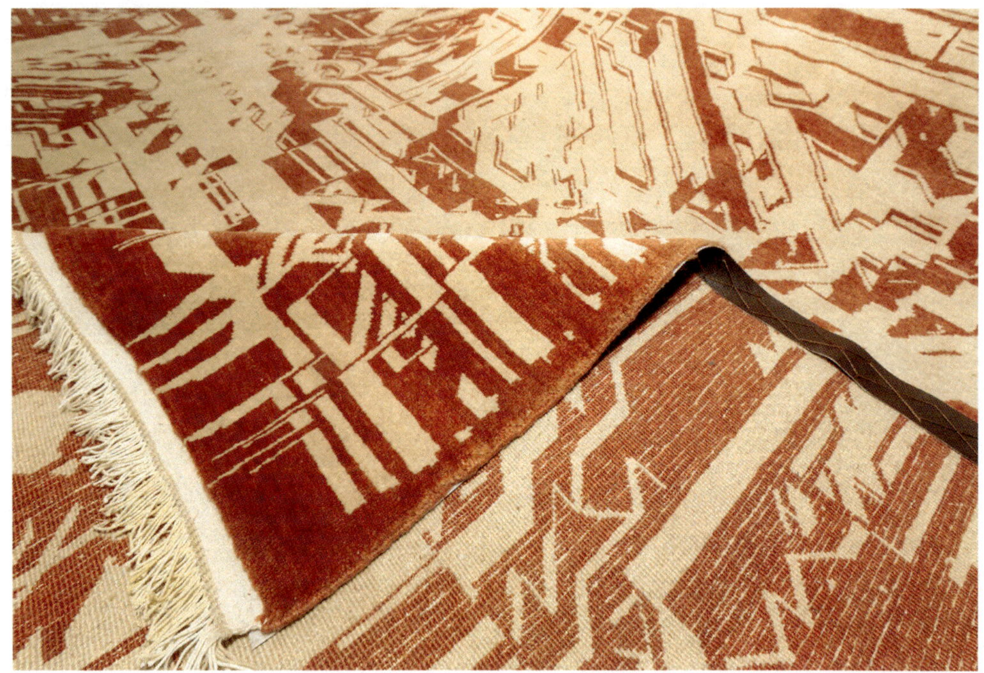

©Rugture

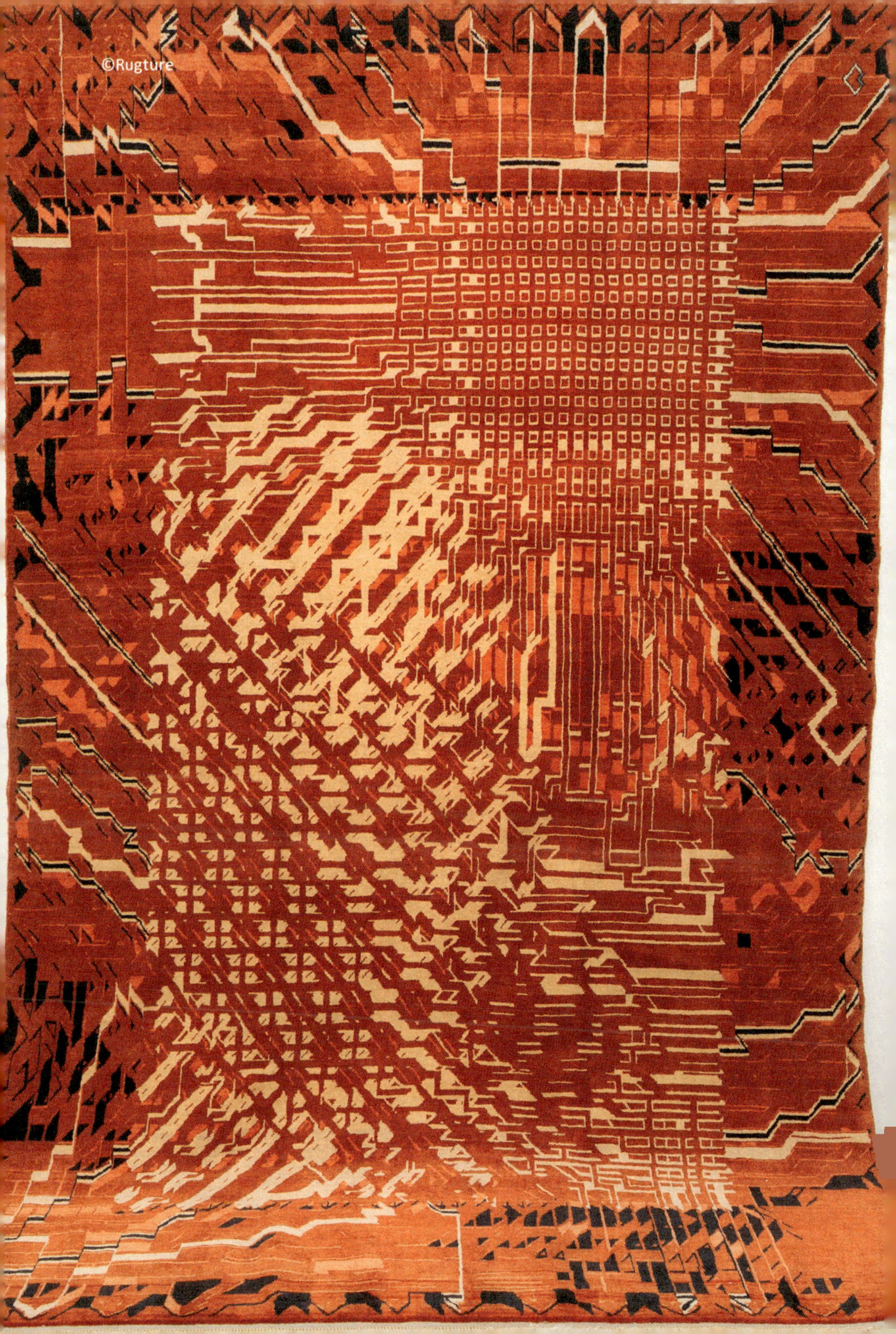
©Rugture

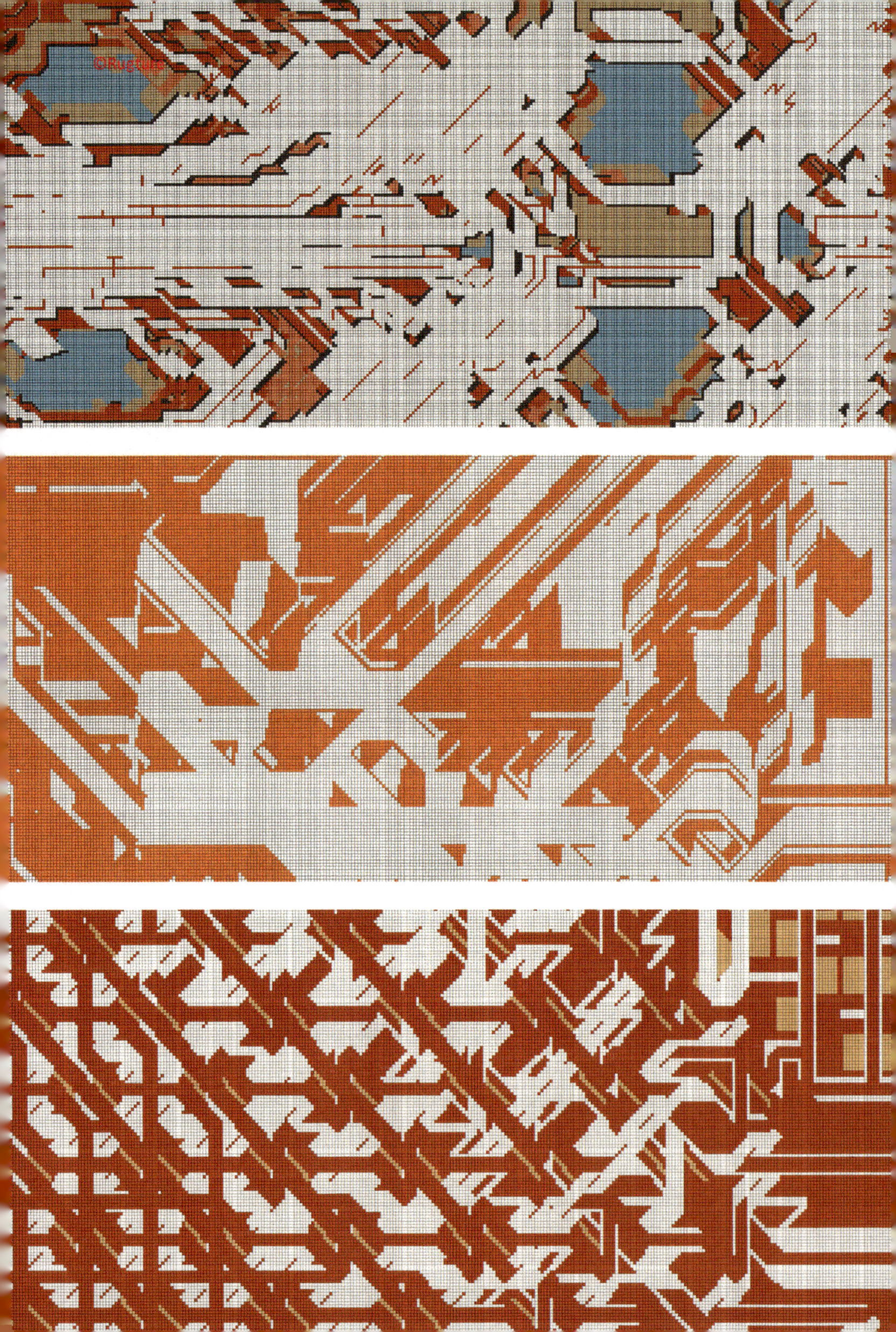

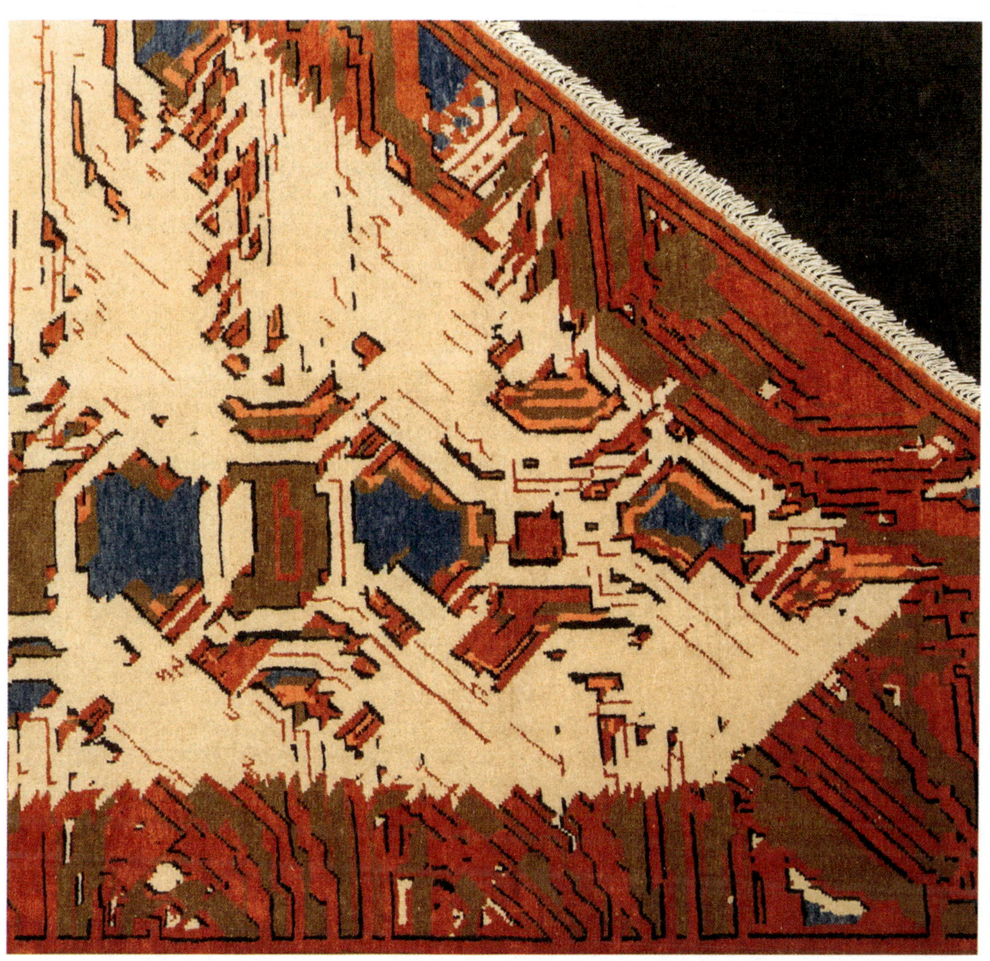

Once a color combination has been selected, the rugs' design is converted to a pixelated knotting plan. After the knotting plan is printed on paper in the rug's original size, it is sent in rolls to Tabriz. After many steps from the untanned wool to the finished product, the carpet is sent to Vienna for final inspection. Four main collections exist: classic (reinterpretation of classical designs), adaptive (tailor-made design), dynamic (break from rectangular format), and modular (combined hexagonal pieces).

Text by: Kourosh Asgar-Irani

TALK-live transcript

ELEONORA D'ASCENZI: Now I'm going to introduce to all of you, Kourosh Asgar-Irani, founder of "Rugture". Kourosh is an architect who grew up in Vienna but is originally from Iran. He is now based between London and Vienna. He learned his skills from a very famous architect, Zaha Hadid. After starting to collect antique rugs, he developed an interesting technique to apply parametric design tools - to the design of rug patterns, connecting digital design techniques and traditional persian fabrication patterns. This is how the cultural section of "Rugture" was founded. So, Kourosh, thank you for being here. The floor is yours.

KOUROSH ASGAR-IRANI: Thank you. "Rugture" actually started after I realized the huge potential to combine my architectural expertise with my passion of ancient rugs and antiques.

There is a specific type of rug, produced in the 19th century that inspired me to start "Rugture" - these are antique Heriz/Serapi rugs.

What makes them so fascinating is their complex geometric shapes - if you take a closer look at them, they remind you of computed graphics with their pixelated appearance. They are however abstract representations of plants and greens - so much beauty and complexity that inspired me to bring geometrical representation to a new level and create a new type of rug that uses parametric computer graphics to bring rug design to the 21st century. I aimed to create designs that resemble these patterns but in a digital way. I started designing a series of intricate rug patterns. However, to make my designs a reality I had to find the perfect place for production. I wanted to make the persian heritage of rug production part of "Rugture", so I started collaborating with workshops near the historical towns of Tabriz, where my father is from and Heriz, which is the place these antique rugs were originally produced. In some ways my work with "Rugture" allowed me to reconnect with the country I was born in.

My first collection, the "Classic Collection", was showcased at the 2019 Salone del Mobile in Milan. For this collection I decided to focus on a new interpretation of very classic Persian rug designs. The composition follows certain rules: you have the medaillon in the center of the rug, followed by one fourth of the medaillon on the four corners and a frame around it (Image 1). This is how it all started. What I really love about these rugs is that the patterns never repeat themselves (Image 2). You could own these rugs for 30 or 40 years and would still be able to find something new. Of course I also wanted to try designs without a medallion and these are the results (Image 3). When you look closely at the details, you also notice here that not a single pattern is repeated. All pieces however contain the typical framing.

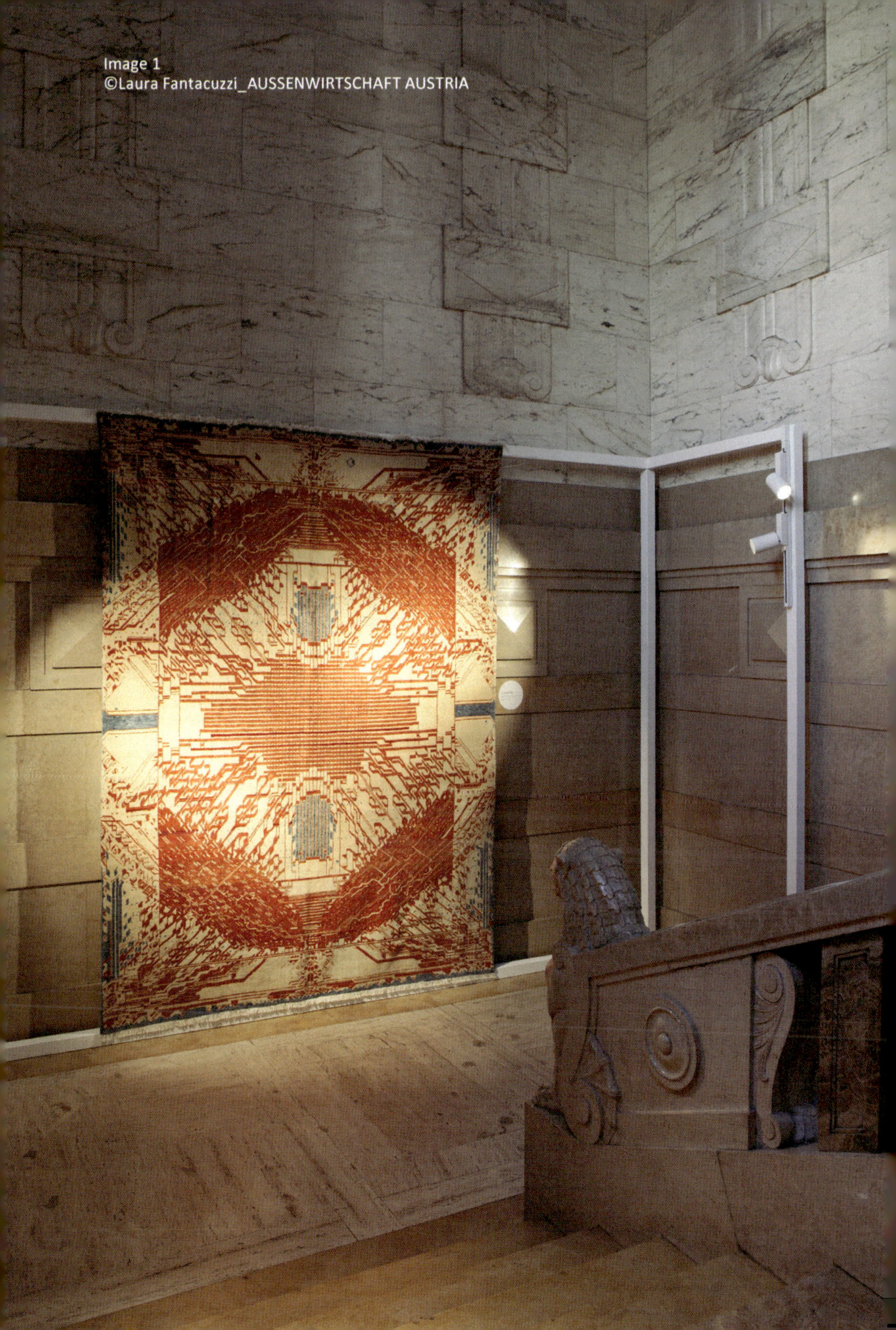

Image 1
©Laura Fantacuzzi_AUSSENWIRTSCHAFT AUSTRIA

In my next collection, the "Adaptive collection" I started creating rugs that are custom made for each space (Image 4). All surrounding parameters like light, walking paths, position of furniture can be implemented for pattern generation, bringing adaptive rug design to its next level.

As you can see in this rug (Image 5), the designs evolved from center medaillons, and I started placing attractors in different corners of the rug, such as on the upper right corner in this example, to see what kind of patterns would be generated.

Looking at some of these adaptive patterns, they sometimes remind me of parametric urban design city planning projects I used to work on.

In this rug (Image 6), you can see how one design evolves across three different stages. What is fascinating about it is that you almost remove the manual control over pattern generation.

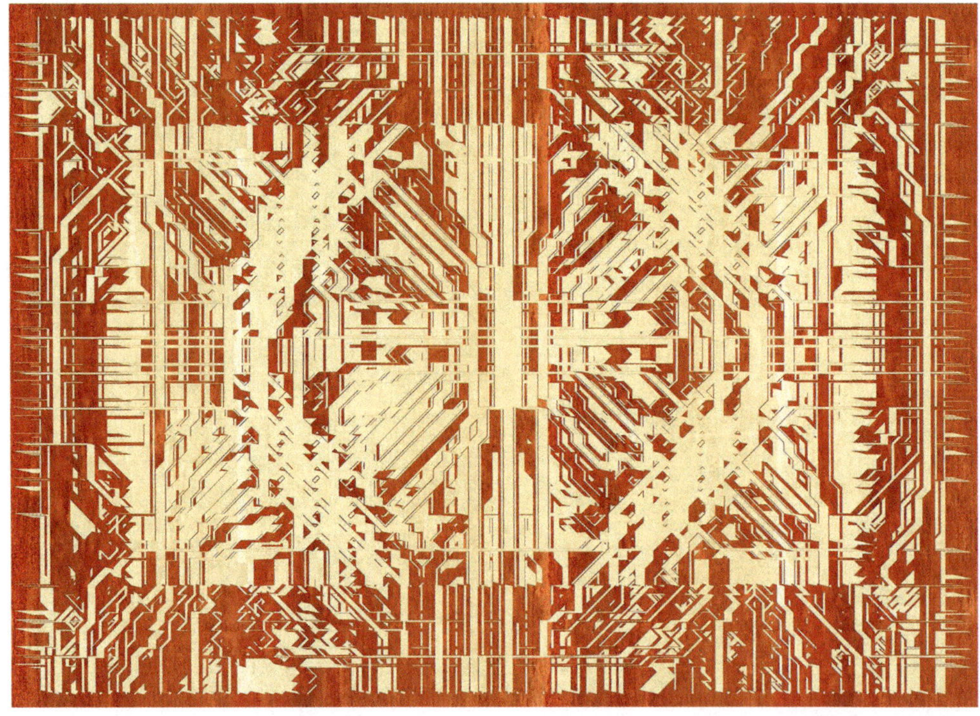

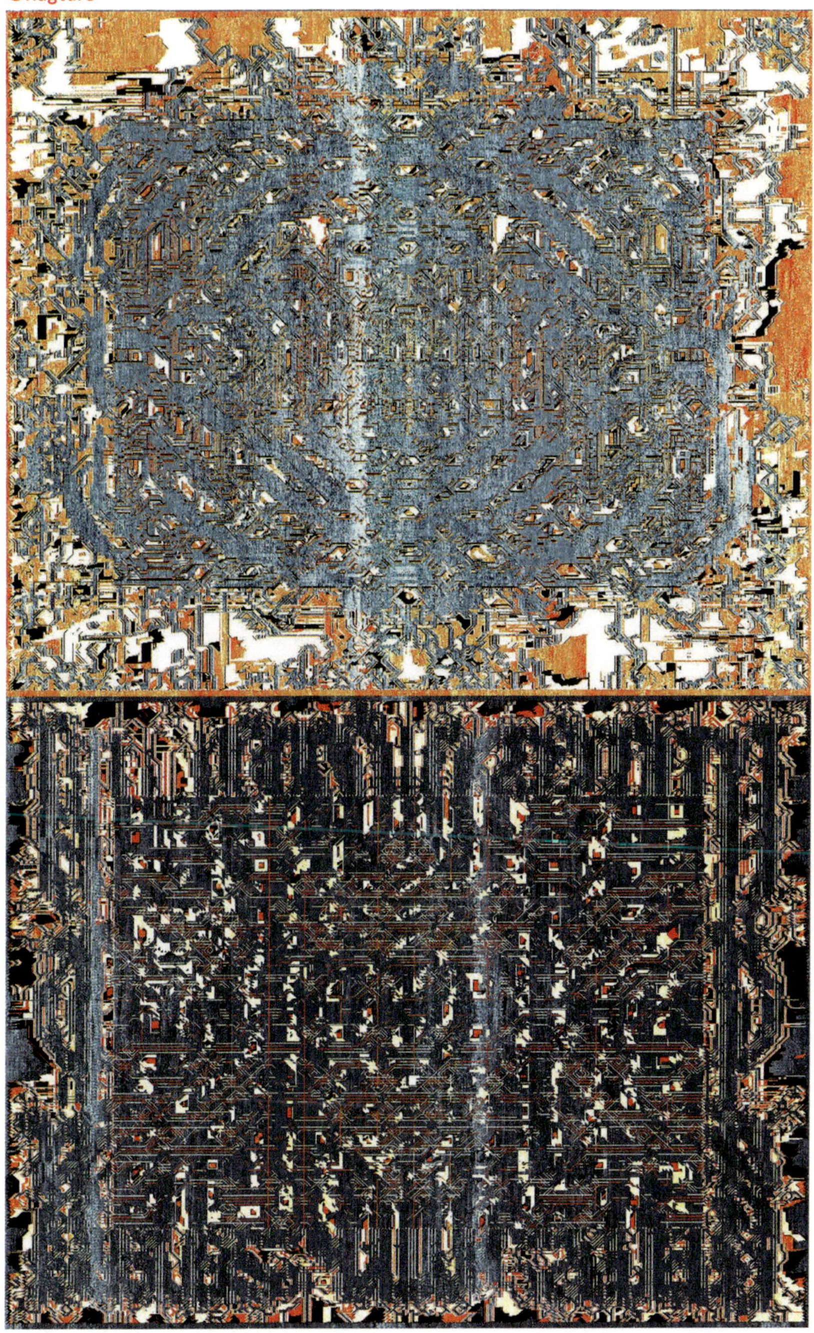

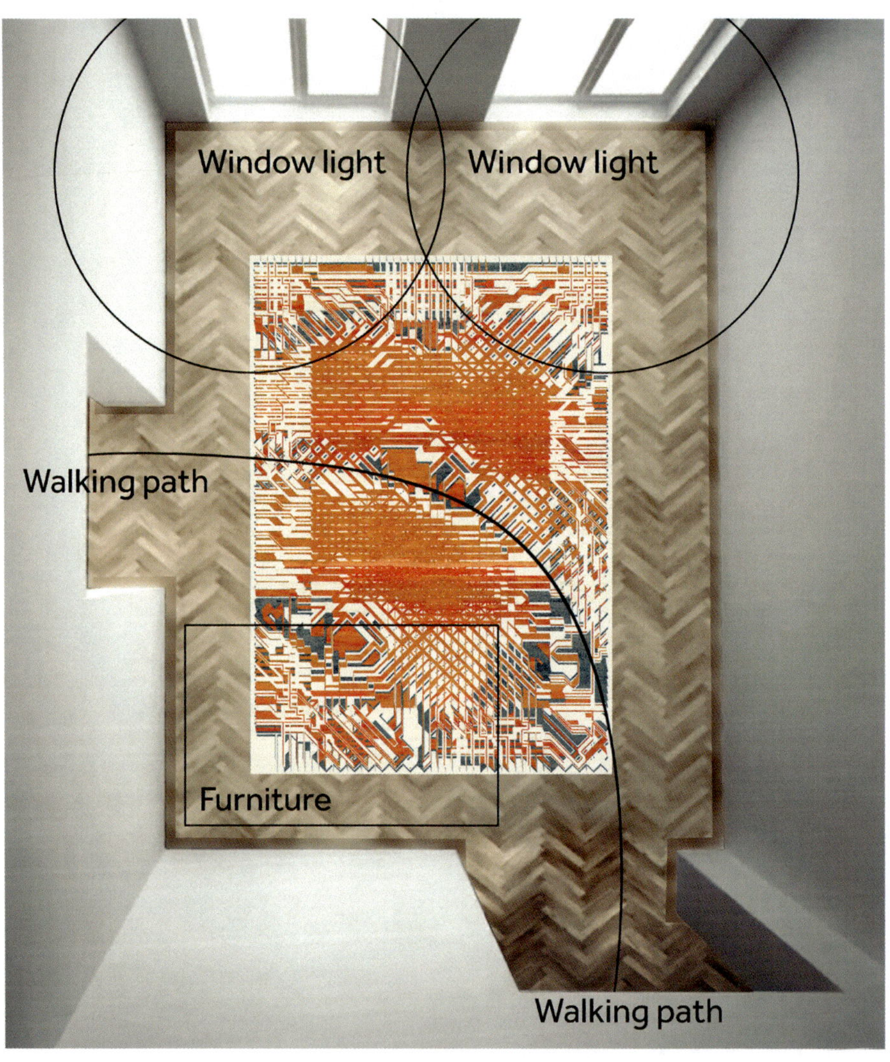
Window light
Window light
Walking path
Furniture
Walking path

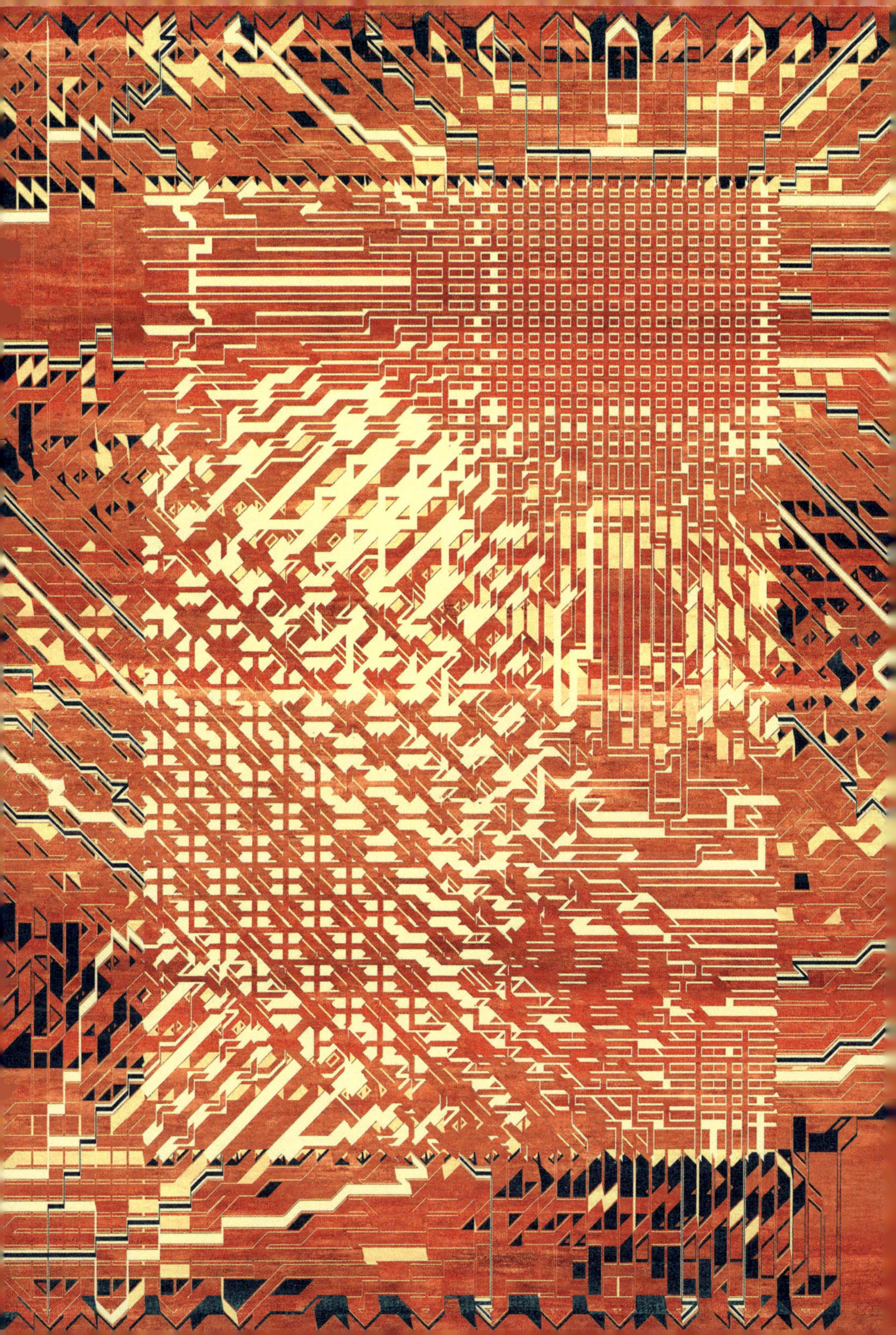

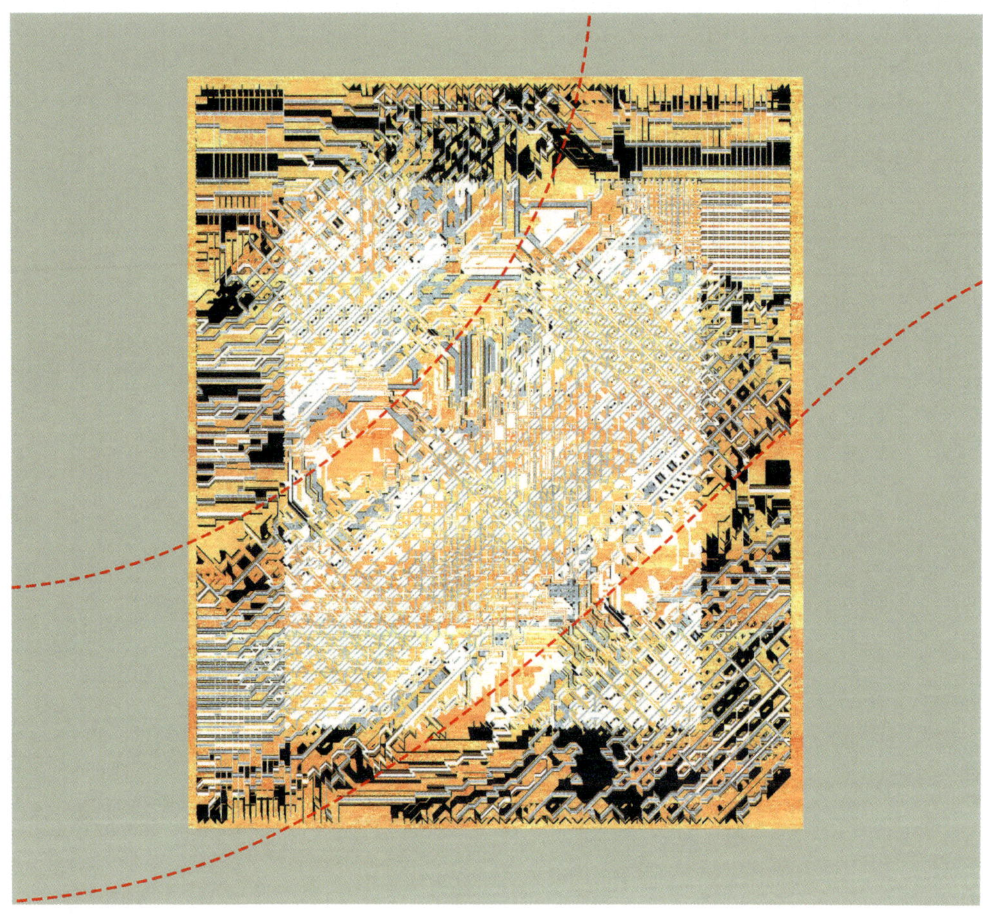

The following animation (Image 7) shows how adaptive patterns are generated. This specific rug was designed for one of my rooms in my flat in Vienna. The pattern follows the room layout of two doors, a clearly visible walking path, the furniture and also the light accessing the room from its two windows.

With the "Dynamic Collection" (Image 8), I started to break free from rectangular shapes to start adding a more dynamic touch. The collection keeps the adaptive patterns, and the rugs ability to evolve around external parameters.

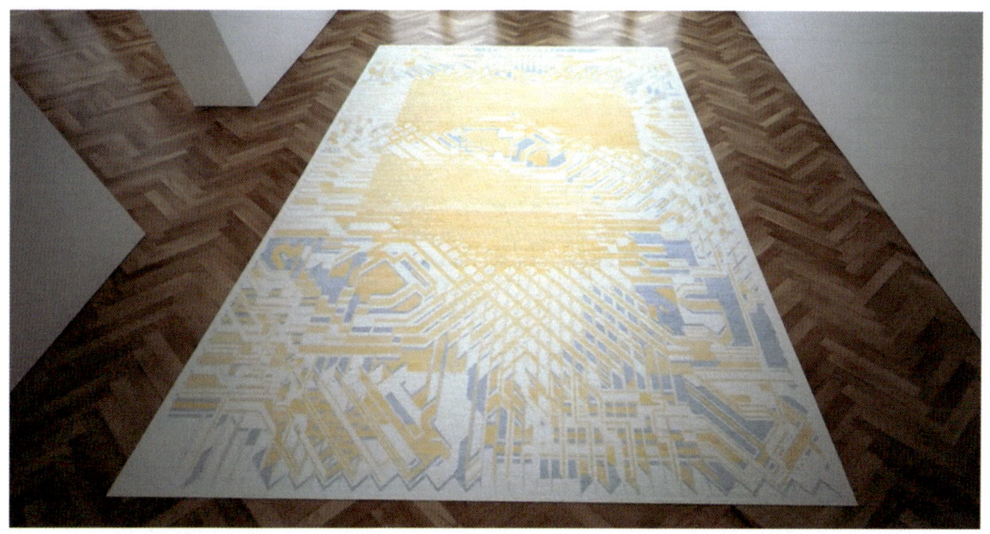

Image 7
©VC Media Ltd (Vincent Cui Studio)

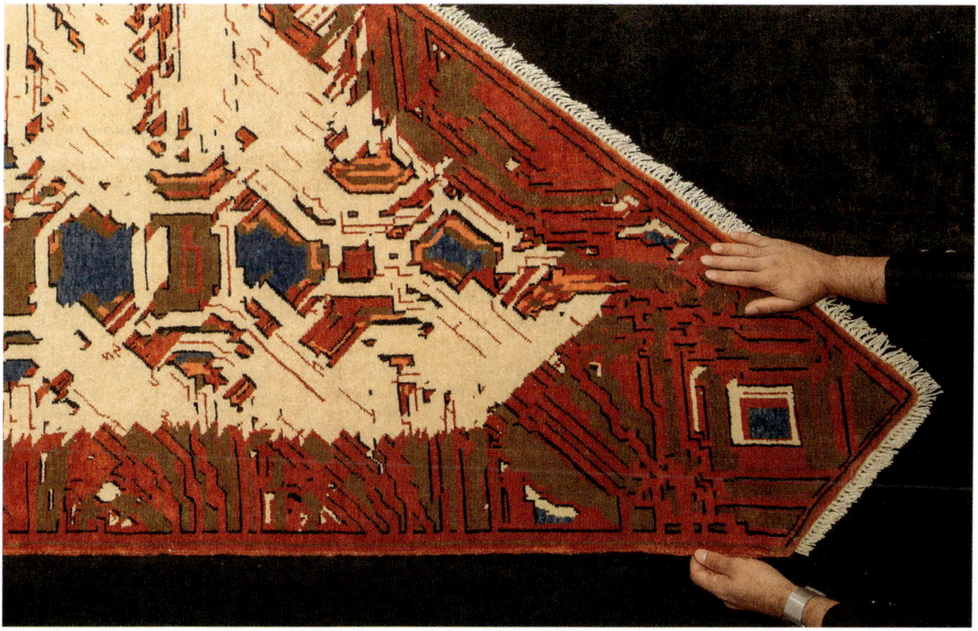

Image 8
©VC Media Ltd (Vincent Cui Studio)

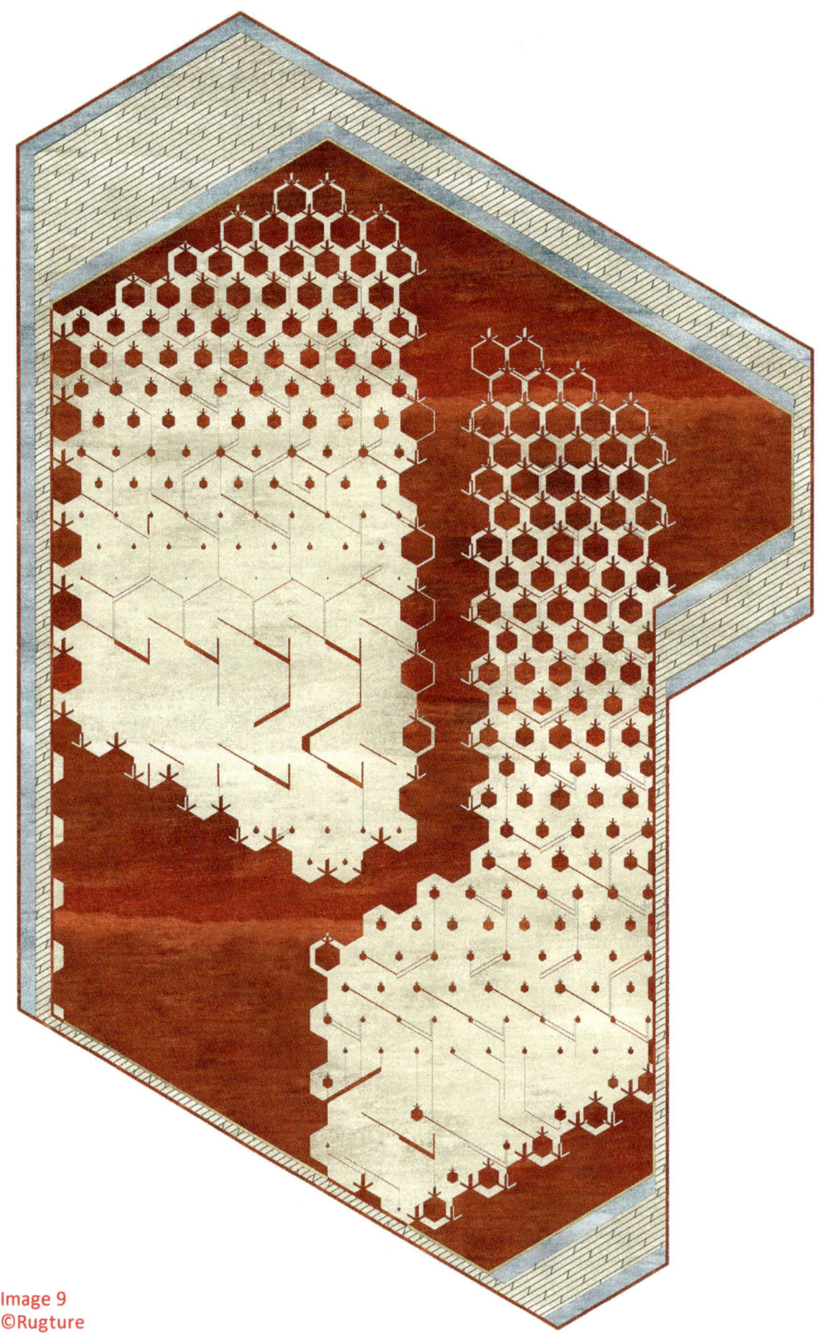

Image 9
©Rugture

This rug (Image 9) is a great example of adaptivity, where the pattern evolves around Armenian pomegranate rugs. The pattern is generated with stylised and abstracted pomegranates, very common for rugs from that area.
In my fourth collection "Modular Collection", I focused on modularity (Image 10) - smaller pieces that can be connected to fit the requirements of a room. It breaks away from the rug being the centerpiece of a space, but can for instance be positioned to connect walking paths to doors or fit into smaller spaces.
All these rugs are handmade, produced with natural dyes and natural wool. Manual fabrication is really important in my view to combine state of the art, generative design and ancient manufacturing methods.

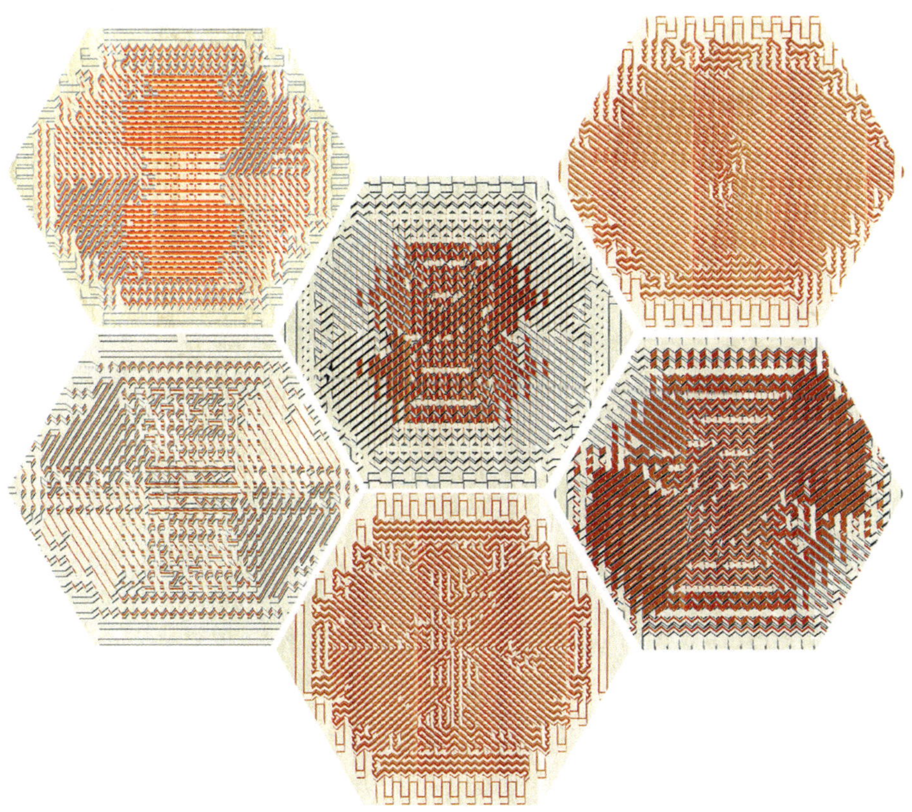

Image 10
©Rugture

However, I am also experimenting with new fabrication methods, such
as robotic fabrication that allows for more spatial constructions, bringing
classic rugs to a next level, not possible with manual fabrication.
One of my projects creates three dimensional woven sculptures produced by
robotic fabrication methods. These produce intricate patterns but weave them
to become complex spatial sculptures, furniture or even complete spaces.
I am very excited about experimenting with these three dimensional shapes
to produce furniture or interior design pieces. This is only the beginning.
Thank you so much for listening.
ELEONORA D'ASCENZI: Thank you Kourosh. It was great learning more about
your approach, your current collections and future projects. It is amazing to
see how generative design can be applied to disrupt more traditional fields.

ELEONORA D'ASCENZI: I have a question about "Rugture". How and to what extent has your cultural background influenced your project? What is the average timing for the realization of the projects, from design to production?

KOUROSH ASGAR-IRANI: This is a great question. My cultural background has definitely shaped my understanding of Persian culture, its antiques and heritage. This has led to my deep interest in rugs. You need to remember that "Persian Carpets" have a massive global reputation. They are an important brand with huge recognition, but unfortunately the industry in Iran is suffering right now. Growing up in a home full of carpets made me think about how rugs could be interpreted. Combined with my architectural background and my love for antiques this led me to founding "Rugture". It all started with the idea of having my rugs produced in places where the design inspiration comes from, to create something in an area full of heritage as close to an "original piece" as possible. This means that if I were to work on a reinterpretation of Mughal rugs, I would also have them produced in India. That said, it is also interesting to work with different workshops and production facilities. I am now starting to experiment with workshops in Afghanistan for instance - curious to see where this leads me. In terms of the duration, each square meter takes about one month in production. It is a very time consuming production method, but it can be optimized. To give you an example, the piece shown at Salone del Mobile (Image 1) took about six months to be produced. The three pieces shown at the London Design Fair took about 8 months in production, but they were produced simultaneously, which is so much quicker. You definitely need patience in this business, but you are also creating custom made, bespoke pieces - here to last for generations to come. The pieces made in Iran are definitely something special.

ELEONORA D'ASCENZI: There is also one more question about your background and your process: is there any relationship between choosing colors and your background culture?

KOUROSH ASGAR-IRANI: In terms of colors, not actually. Many rug designers like to experiment with bright and flashy colors. This is something I find interesting and I do plan to implement more color experimentation in the near future. At this point I believe it is important for my rugs to match the color palettes of antique rugs, to bring out the heritage with all natural dye colors.

"Una comunità
ci serve.

Marco Aime

craft 4.0 for
COMMUNITY

Unfold & Tim Knapen

The Unfold studio, founded in 2002 by Claire Warnier and Dries Verbruggen after they graduated from the Design Academy Eindhoven, develops projects that investigate new ways of creating, manufacturing, financing and distributing in a changing context. A context in which we see aspects of the pre-industrial craft economy merging with high tech industrial production methods and digital communication networks. A context that has the potential to shift power, from industrial producers and those regulating infrastructure to the individual designer and the consumer. Tim Knapen (1982, Belgium) is an artist and designer who likes to play on the edge of the digital and the physical world. He likes to explore the possibilities of merging digital technology with tactile, real-world experiences.
He runs a studio called "Works of Fiction", in Antwerp, Belgium and teaches at Design Academy Eindhoven.

UNFOLD & TIM KNAPEN

L'ARTISAN ÉLECTRONIQUE

Claire Warnier and Dries Verbruggen (Unfold) in cooperation with Tim Knapen, are working on a project which they call "L'Artisan Électronique". In this research-project they are combining traditional pottery techniques with new digital media.

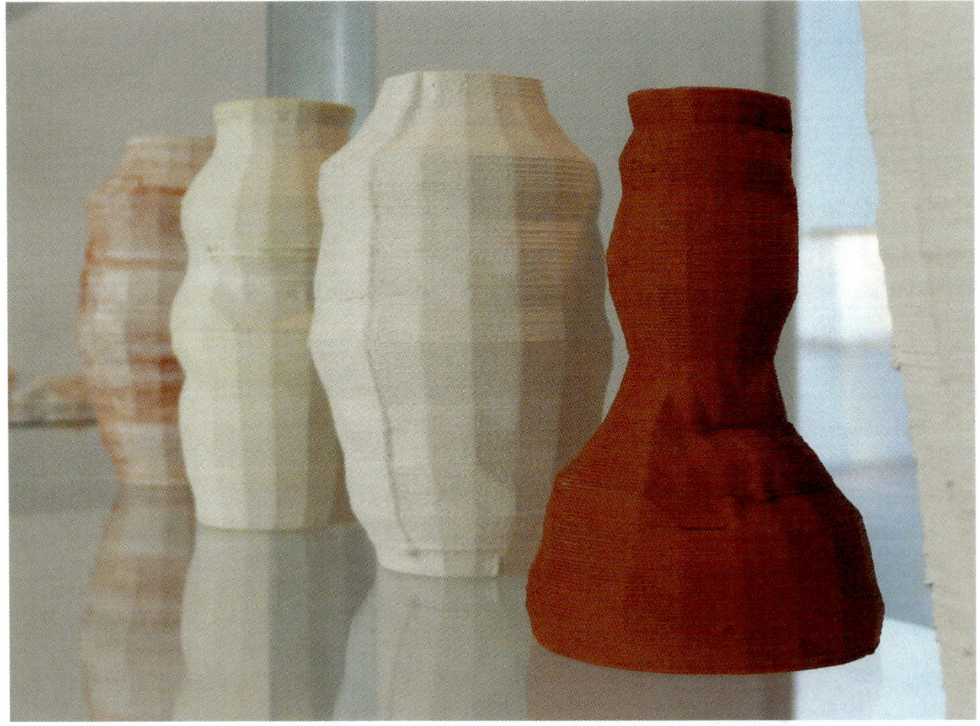

©Unfold

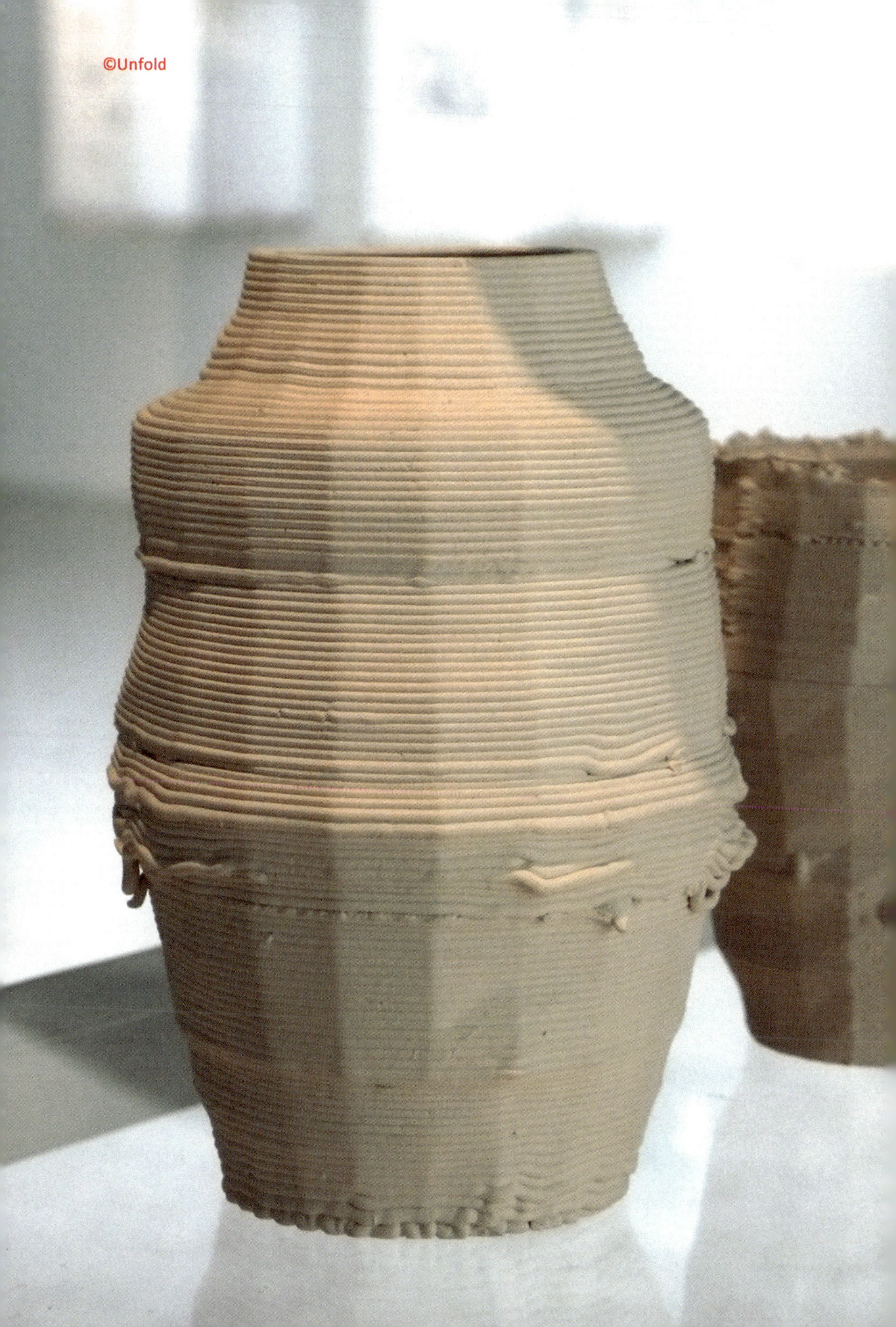
©Unfold

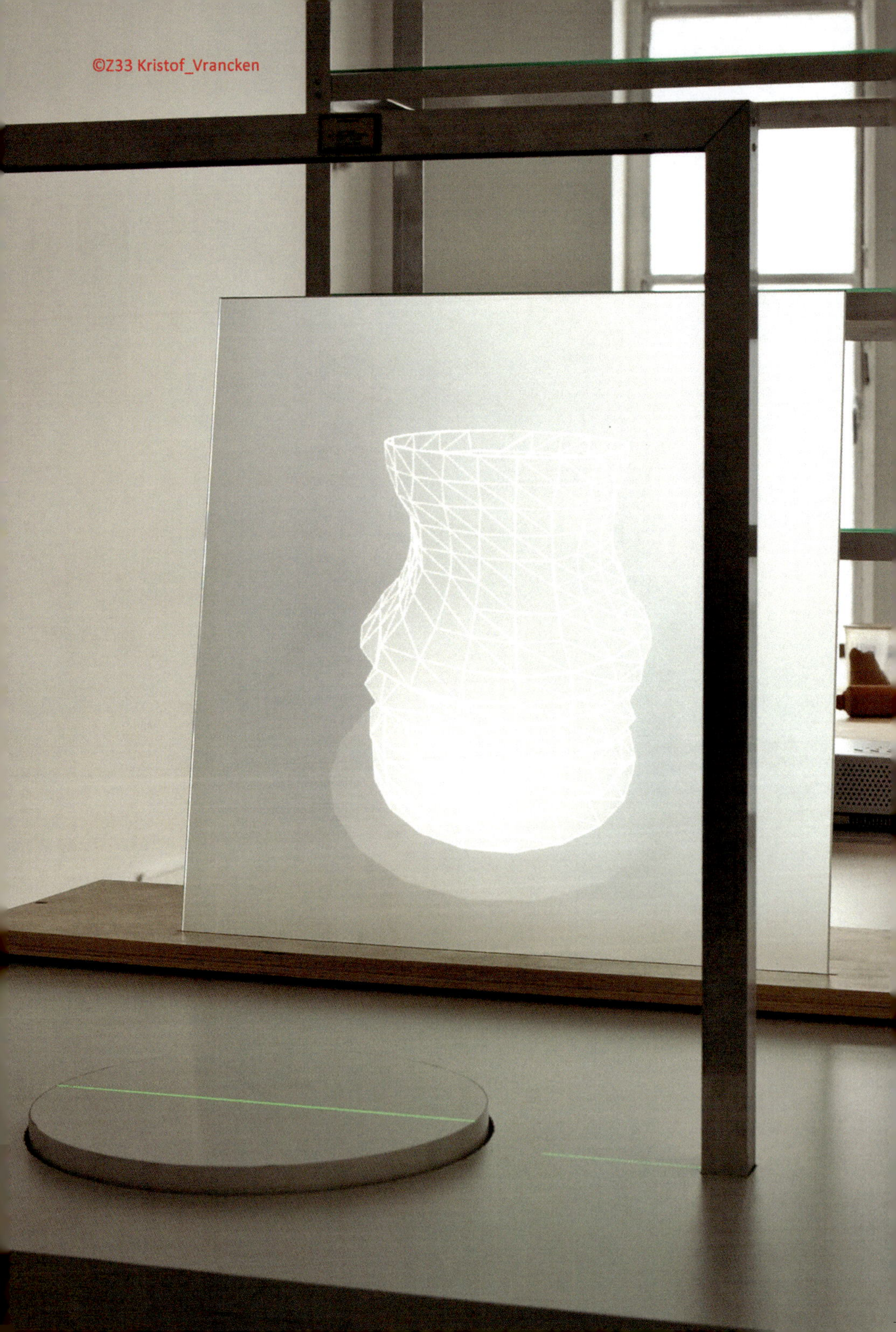

©Z33 Kristof_Vrancken

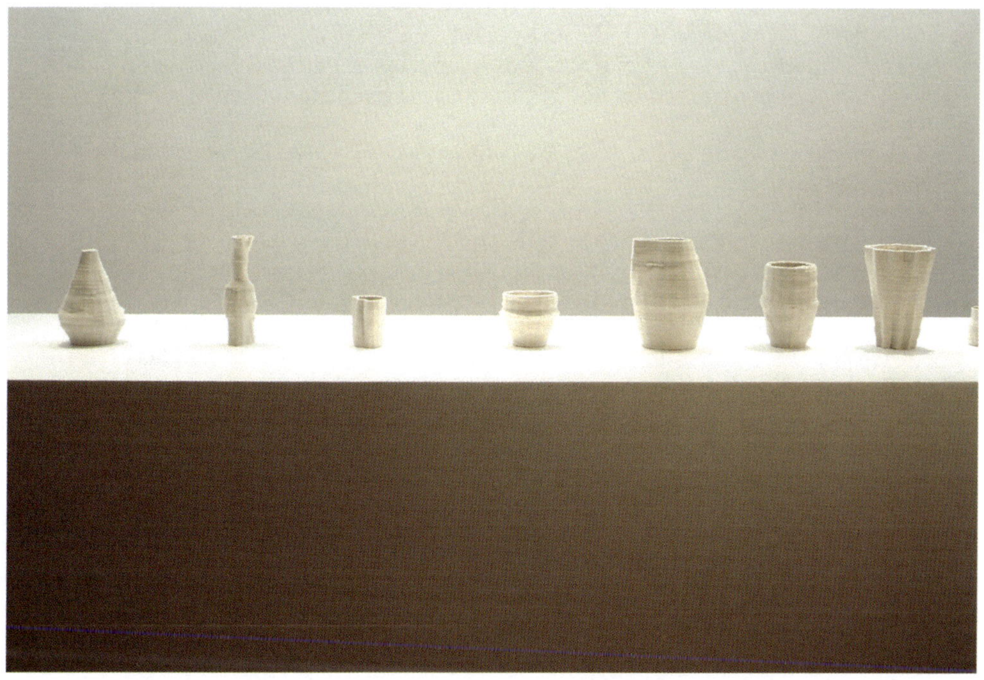

Unfold is fascinated by a new movement that is called "Personal Fabrication", a trend in which we see a shift from mass produced items to locally, personally produced objects. All kinds of tools and services are now available, mostly through the internet, to produce your own digitally designed objects. These tools vary from open-source DIY 3D-printers to (online) production services and online communities to distribute your designs.

Text by: Claire Warnier

TALK-live transcript

ELEONORA D'ASCENZI: So, the first designer I'm honored to introduce is Tim Knapen who is going to talk about his project in collaboration with Unfold: "L'Artisan Électronique" which belongs to the section Craft 4.0 for the community. Tim runs a studio in Belgium and he teaches at the Design Academy in Eindhoven. In this project pottery, which is one of the oldest techniques, is combined with the new digital media by using "a virtual pottery wheel". This project is part of a new movement called "Personal Fabrication", with a shift from mass production to local and personal production. But let's start with him.
Tim, thank you for being here. We are curious to know a little bit more about your concept ideas.
TIM KNAPEN: Thank you, Eleonora. Hello, everybody. I am Tim and I made this installation "L'Artisan Électronique" about 10 years ago, maybe 11. I made this project with Unfold, a design studio in Antwerp. I am a designer working in Antwerp and they are a separate studio, also working in Antwerp. We are good friends and we share a lot of interests. We sometimes jointly create projects and this is one of the projects we did together. So, the idea of "L'Artisan Électronique" that you can see here (Image 1) is a kind of traveling version of the installation. The idea was to create a virtual potter's studio in which people could digitally create shapes. The installation has traveled quite a lot and it has seen many different shapes. It consists of a few main parts. So first you have the pottery wheel, which is this (Image 2) weird table with the traditional potter's disc, the laser and the screen. The screen is the tool that allows people to create shapes by just holding their hands in front of this laser: we created the system that would detect your hand in space, which now is super common in computer games.
But before that, this did not exist. So, we created this (Image 3) very bright laser with the warning sign above it - that is telling you not to stare into it - and it is able to detect your hands in space. Then, you could manipulate this cylinder on the screen and create your pot, or vase or whatever you wanted.

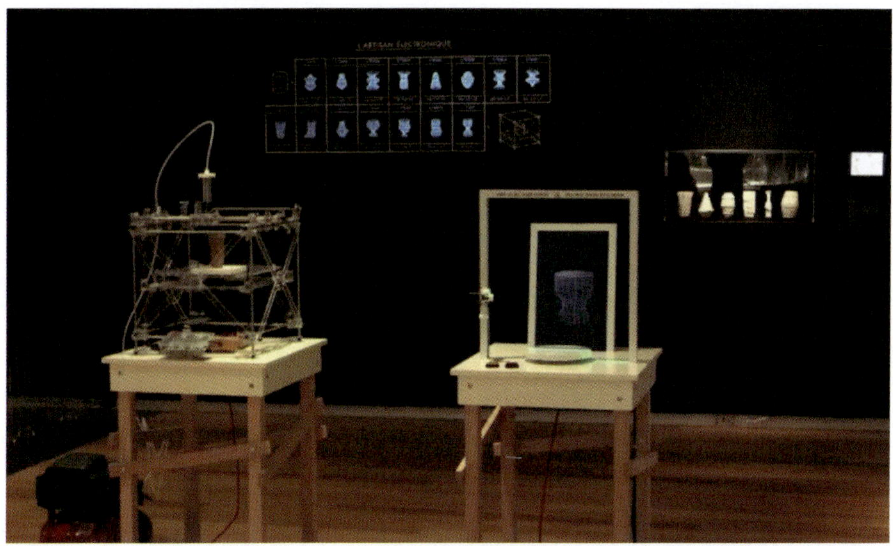

Image 1
©Unfold

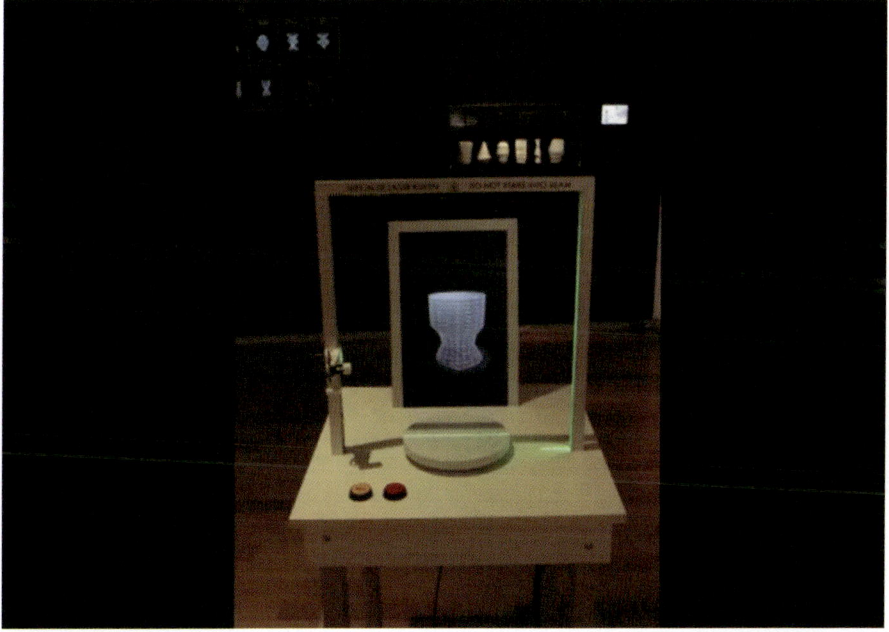

Image 2
©Unfold

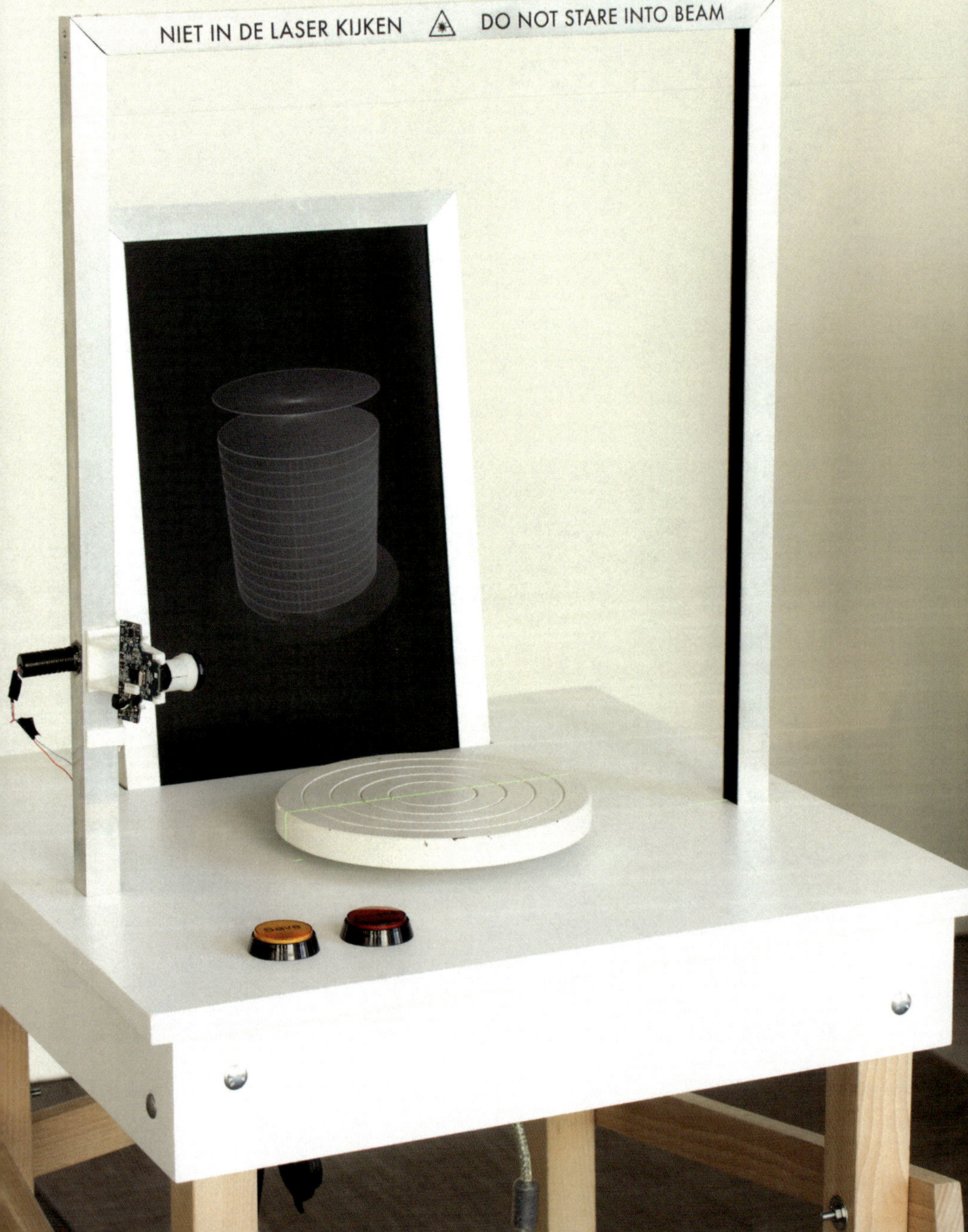

NIET IN DE LASER KIJKEN
DO NOT STARE INTO BEAM

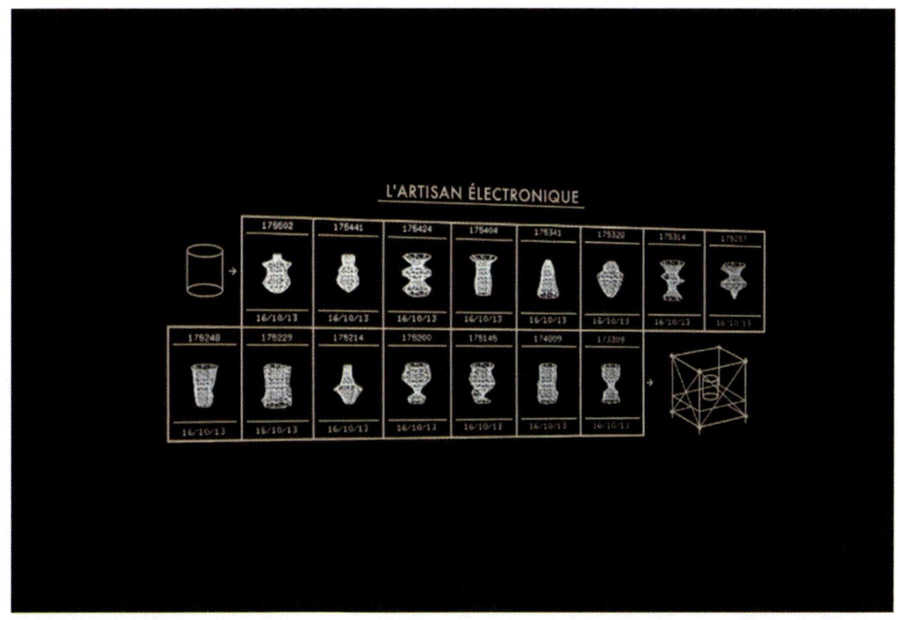

Image 4
©Unfold

And then it would end up on this display (Image 4) on the wall, which is just
a sticker on the wall with a projection and it would also show you the other
objects that people had made before you. So, you can see there was all these
kind of polygon faces. That's the printer (Image 5). That's after your object
has been saved into our system. Your design was printed on this modified 3D
printer and then it would end up in the cupboard. And so, we have these 3D
ceramic prints of these very ugly low polygon faces that have travelled with
the exhibition.
I would like to say something about the travelling set up because, you know,
big installations don't like to travel the world since they cannot be exhibited
anywhere because nobody wants to pay for the shipping. But this was the
original installation at Z33, which is the Art Center in Belgium, and they
commissioned this project.

So, they asked to Unfold to make something for this exhibition. And at this point me and Dries were very interested in this new emerging movement: the open-source 3D printer. And we wanted to do something with this. Unfold was very interested in ceramics, so we decided to create this digital studio. Since I am an interactive and digital designer, I create a lot of installations and objects that work with computers and electronics, very nerdy and mostly deals with creating tools for visitors to play with, allowing interactivity in the audience. And the whole idea of this thing was to allow you to imagine what a digital-physical way of working could look like. So, if you could imagine someone having a studio and working with real materials and actual textures but at the same time using digital tools in this very merged fluent way, this was our kind of imagined way how this studio could look like (Image 6). You see this little table where the virtual pottery wheel was. Visitors sit at the table and make their pots. And it was a linear process where you have the creation.

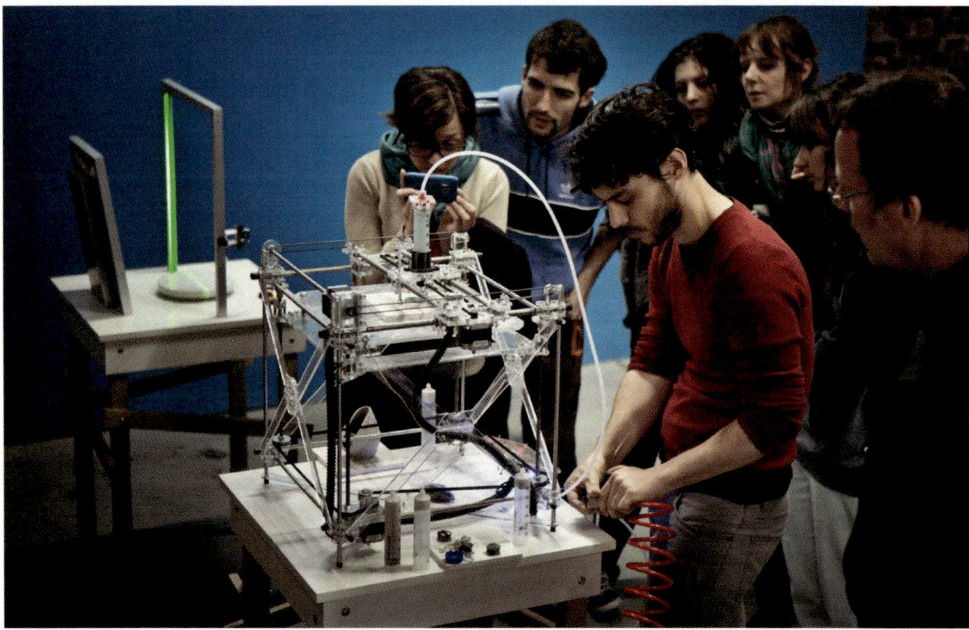

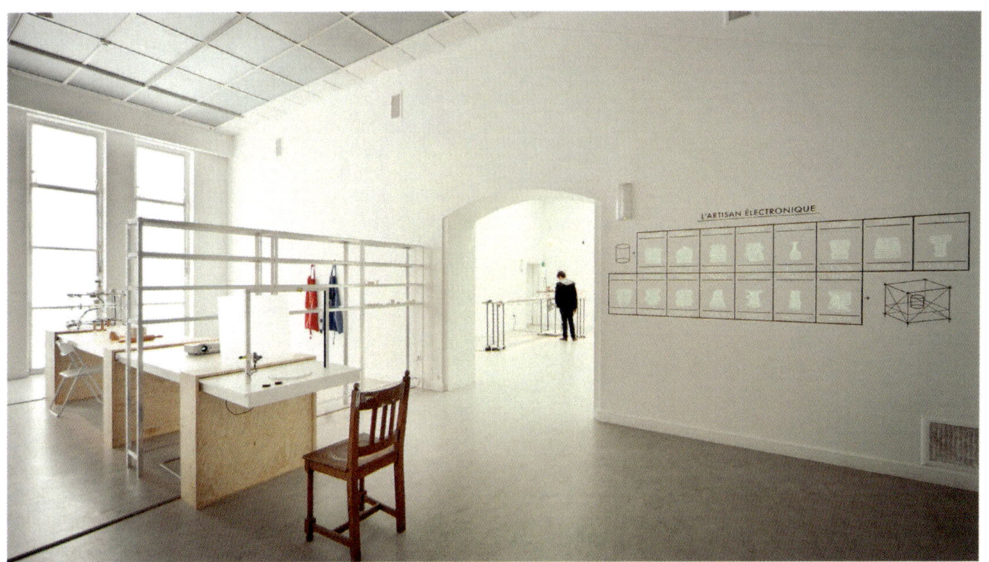

Image 6
©Z33 Kristof_Vrancken

Then you have this kind of cupboard against the wall where the digital objects are being stored, and then you have at the end of the print the output with this 3D printer. So, in the original exhibition, that's what it looks like here (Image 7) this is the original printer. This video (Image 8) is what it looked like if you would touch the laser. So, people could just push into this rotating shape. We tried to create something very intuitive and playful to use, so you wouldn't have to study five years to become a potter before using our digital pottery tool.

ELEONORA D'ASCENZI: Thank you Tim. Thank you for sharing with us your projects and your ideas, as well as for showing us how the human could connect with technology. I think this video framework (Image 9) tells a lot about this aspect.

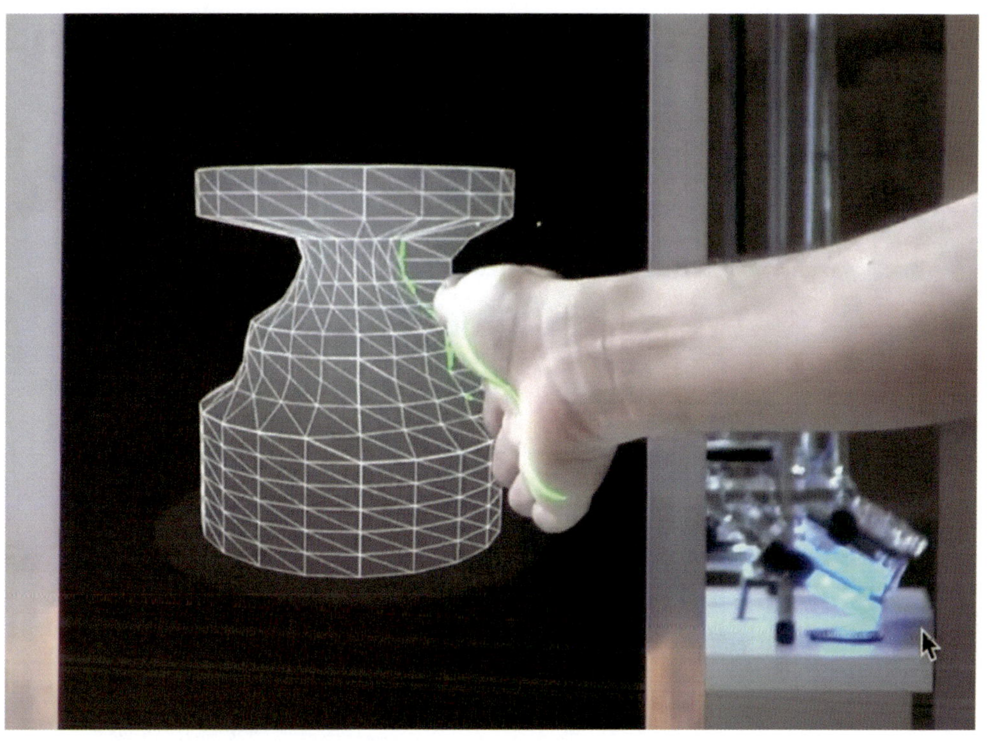

Image 8
©Unfold

QUESTIONS AND ANSWERS

ELEONORA D'ASCENZI: Could you please explain to us if you encountered any difficulties with your project? Could you also please tell us more about the users' experience and their first reaction?

TIM KNAPEN: So, regarding the problems... Well, I already told you about the traveling problem of shipping big tables and stuff. But another issue was when we first built the installation. I think we had about three months-time to come up with something for the exhibition and I remember I met Dries and Claire and we discussed what we would do. At that point, ceramic 3D printing, as far as we knew, did not exist. Nobody was doing anything like this. I believe that in Belgium there were in total two 3D printers at that time and Dries told me he wanted to do the ceramic printing. I am a bit of a nerd, so I wanted to do this interactive part and we split up the work. I remember I said to Dries "we have three months time and we've never printed ceramics. I don't know if this is going to work." I built my prototype of the laser scanner, and I was testing it at home and after a week or two, I had a good prototype. And I asked Dries "How far along are you and is this ever going to work?" and he arrived with this little Tupperware box at my place with just tiny printed ceramic cubes, super messy and dirty. But they were extremely beautiful. I was so happy, and I said: "Ok, we still have two months to finish this and we can start imagining how it's going to work after this first test". But I remember that the big hurdle for me was to believe that we could do it. However, literally within two weeks, he had a super crappy prototype that worked. And then I knew that everything was going to be fine. After that, we did not have any issues, it was a very smooth project. We created some software, we created some hardware and we set it up.

And regarding the people's reaction... I think you can see it a little bit in the photos that I showed of the first exhibition. I always try to create a kind of playful situation in an exhibition to be able to start exploring the possibilities of a tool. So, I wanted to create this experience for the people who visited the exhibition. That was the big goal. So, if somebody comes to the exhibition and does not feel like a little child who wants to play with my toys, then I feel I have lost the game. People see lasers, put their hands inside and you have captured their imagination. And then they start playing with the cylinder. And this is good.

There is one other thing concerning the reaction that I thought was interesting. There was a very positive reaction from people who saw this as a movement, I think, from making technology a bit more tactile and physical. But from the traditional ceramic's world, there were a lot of negative people who said "this is not real ceramics. Ceramics are made with hands and getting yourself dirty without robots". I think nowadays there are so many people experimenting with 3D printed ceramics. It has almost become an old craft after 10 years.

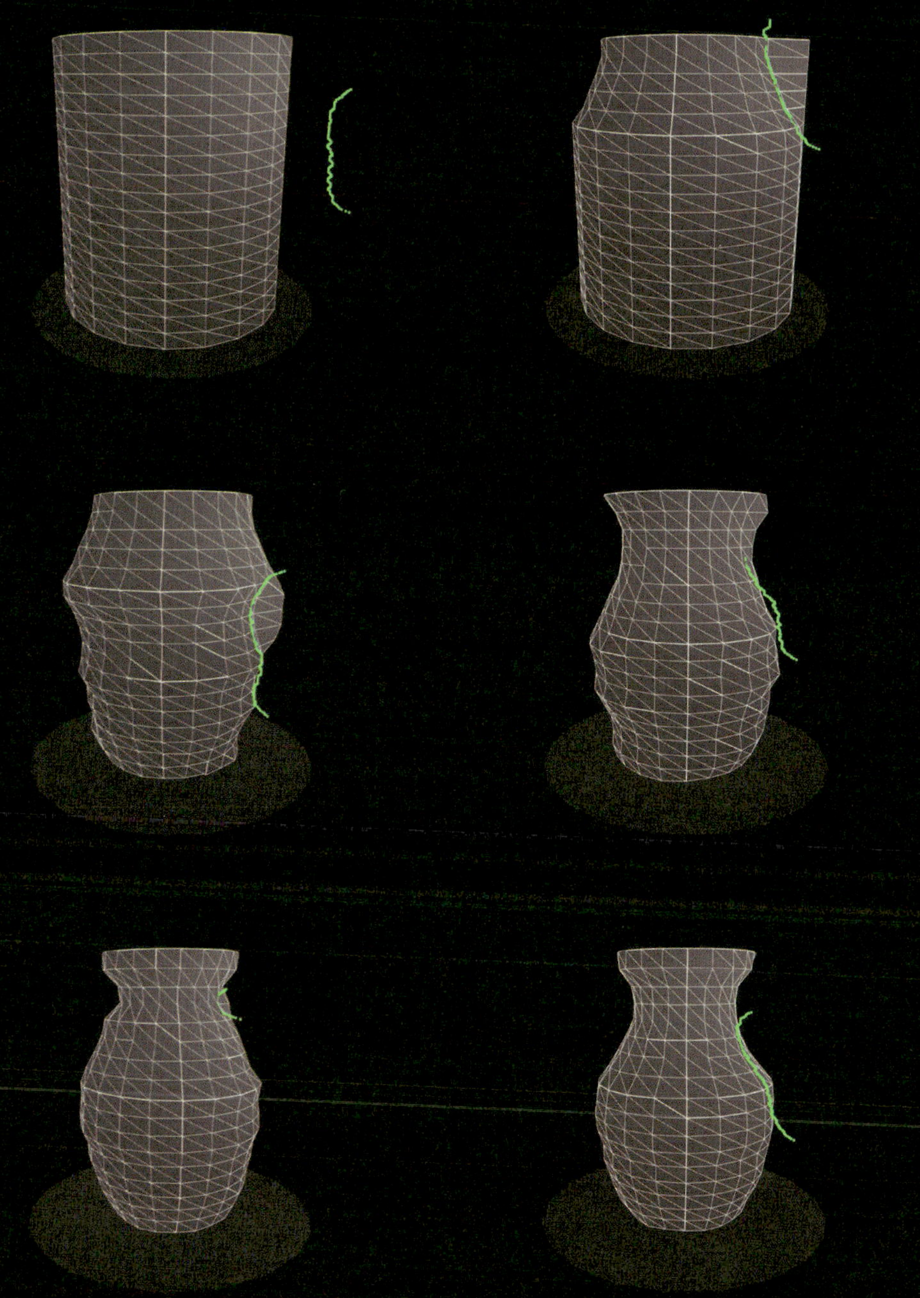

Image 9
©Unfold

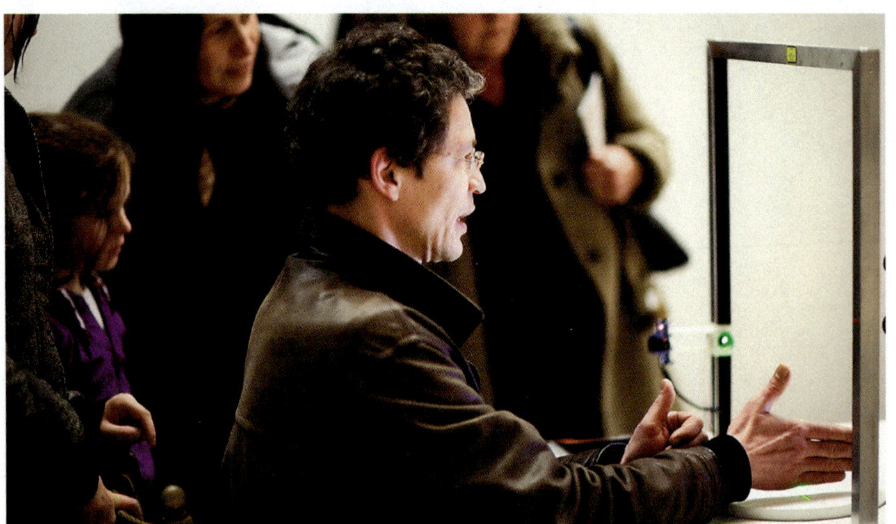

Image 10
©Z33 Liesje Reyskens

ELEONORA D'ASCENZI: Well, there is also another question for you, Tim. What do you think about future applications of new digital technologies especially concerning the relationship between technologies and humans?
TIM KNAPEN: I always feel that people who look at the work, perceive new technology as something magical. But I kind of hate this, I do not believe in this. I believe that technology has always existed and it is just evolving with us. Computers are just things with which I grew up. My father is an electronic engineer, and I always had workshops with little components, and I learned to program when I was a little child. To me, part of "L'Artisan Électronique" is the feeling that you can be close to this technology. So, I do not know, I am not hyped about technology in this way. I think technology is just a tool that you use. And if it is all about technology, then it is a bad project. The example that I always use is when Steve Jobs showed the first iPhone, I was like, "wow, it's amazing": there was this thing, you could touch it and you could move stuff around and… it was magical. But now, if you see people on the train in Rotterdam or wherever, and there are hundreds of people just staring at their phones, it would be crazy if you think "look how amazing it is". Nobody thinks this is amazing anymore, right? And so, there is always this shift with technology that if you believe in the magic of technology, you will lose it in a few years: if that is the point of what you are making, then you are not doing anything, you are not creating anything. Well, not anything interesting to me.
ELEONORA D'ASCENZI: We are losing the main purpose. Thank you.
TIM KNAPEN: To me, yes. That is a personal opinion, of course.

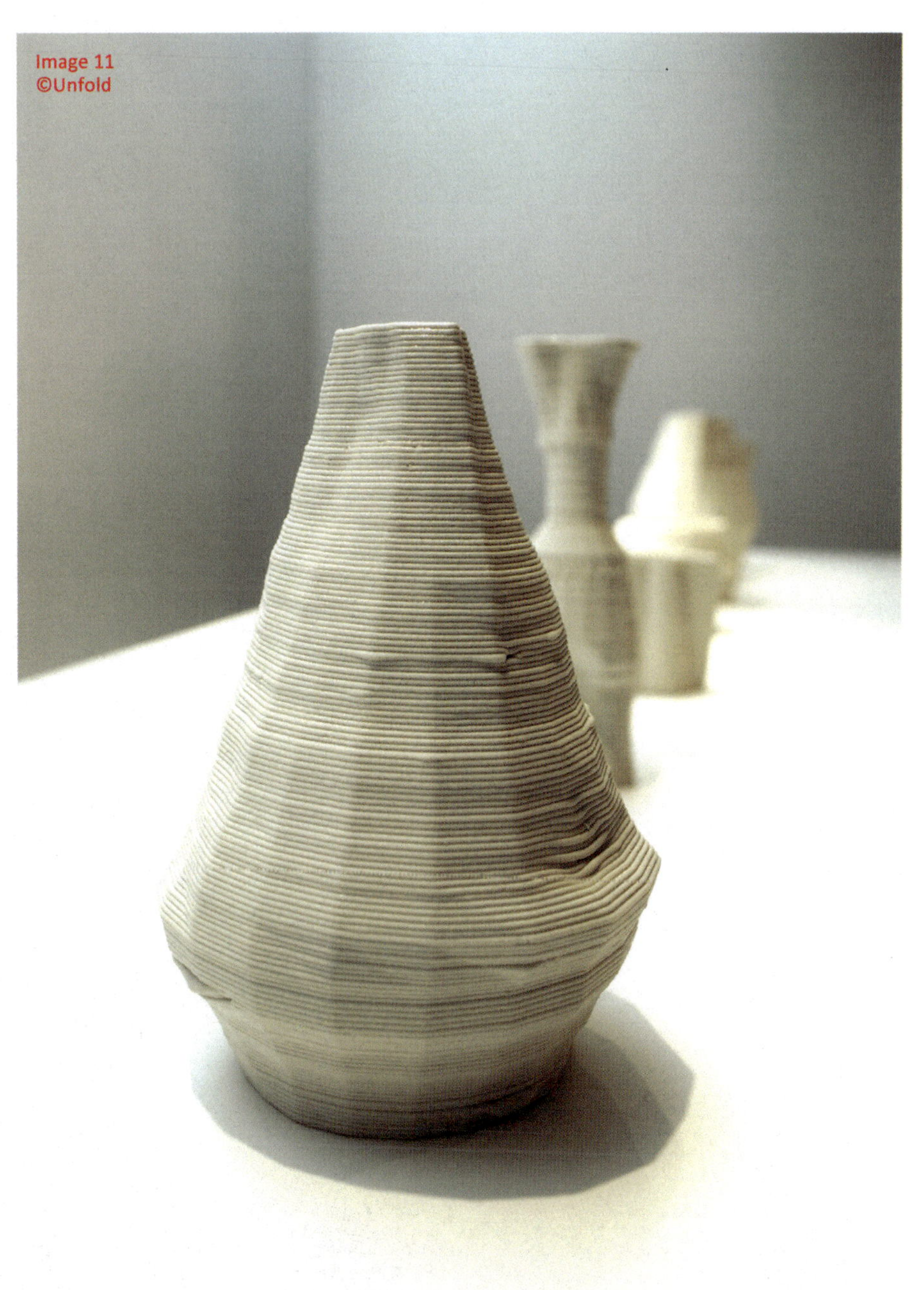

Image 11
©Unfold

Kniterate

"Kniterate" is the brainchild of Gerard Rubio, who 4 years ago started OpenKnit, an open-source knitting machine. The project went viral thanks to its video "Made In The Neighborhood". In the fall of 2015 it was selected to be part of HAX, the first and largest hardware accelerator, in Shenzhen, China. After showing their HAX prototype in Maker Faire Bay they went on to partner with an industrial knitting machine manufacturer, living in the factory the summer of 2016. Since then they have been working with London designers to create samples that show Kniterate's potential.

KNITERATE

THE DIGITAL KNITTING MACHINE

"Kniterate" is a digital knitting machine that wants to change fashion the way desktop 3D printers are revolutionizing manufacturing. It uses yarn to "print" digital clothing files. Via an easy-to-use internet platform, users can design garments from scratch, edit templates or upload their own images and press "knit".

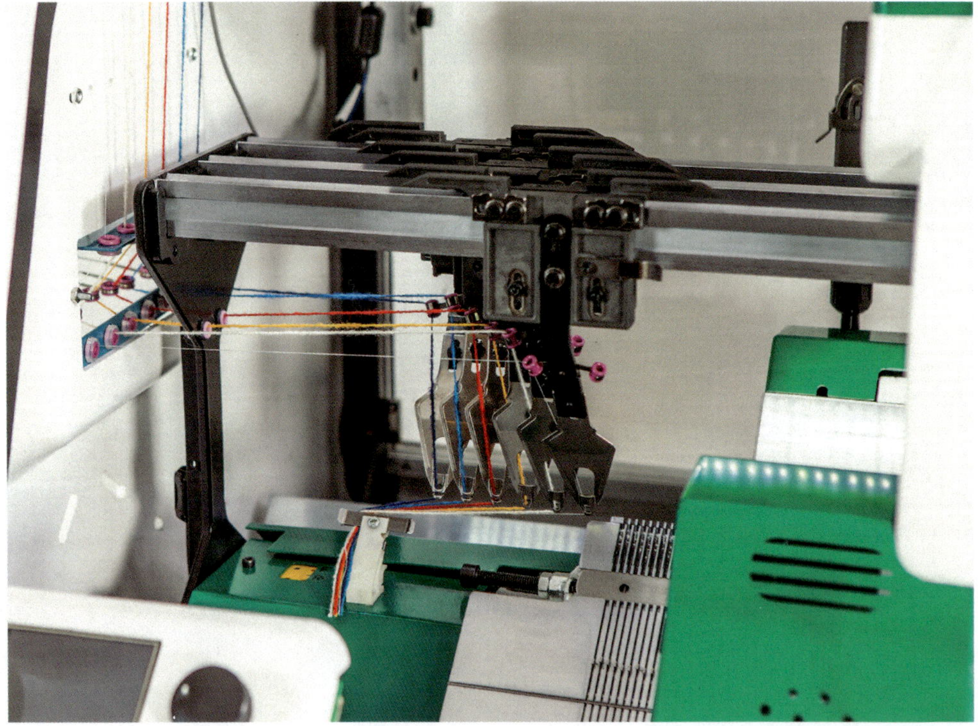

©Kniterate

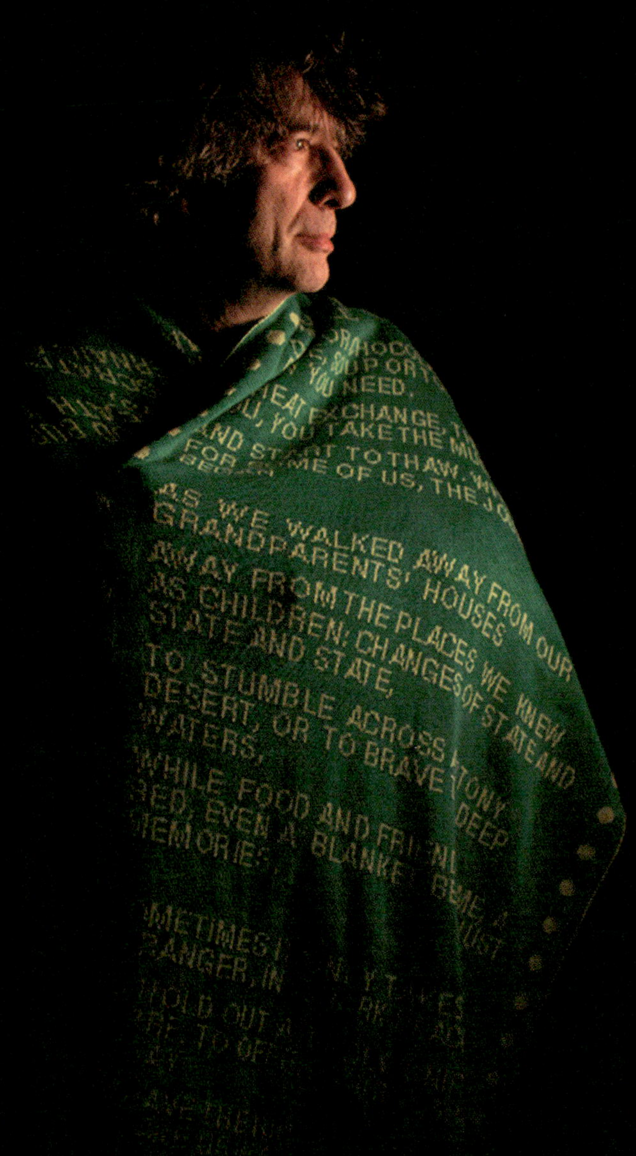

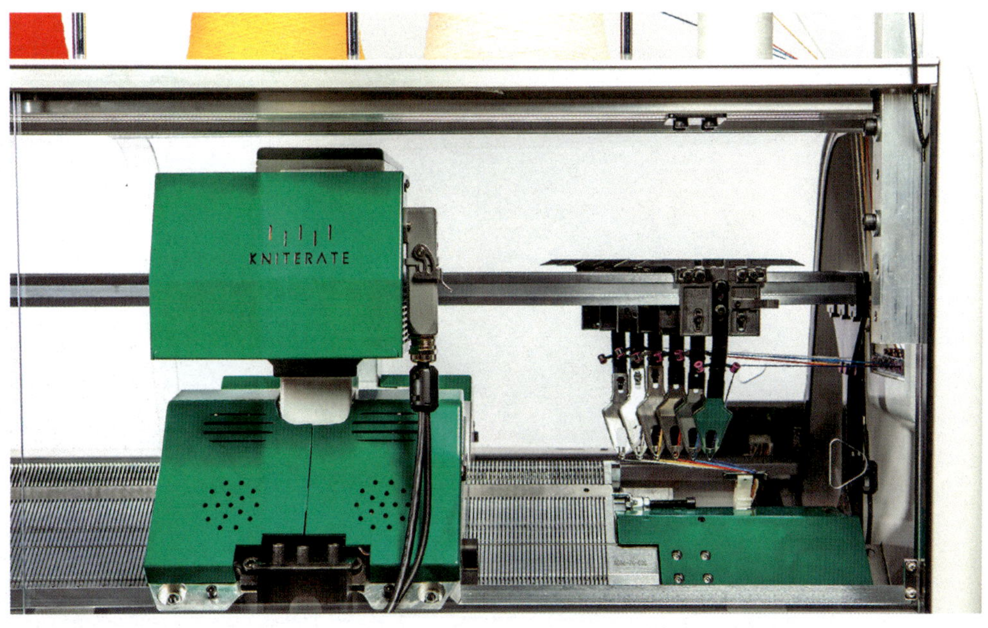

©Kniterate

"Kniterate" provides a tool that makes these kinds of bespoke services more affordable for both the consumer and the maker.
With "Kniterate", clothing is made locally and on demand, and because it is made to shape, there is no waste due to cutting fabrics. "Kniterate" helps fashion designers avoid the long lead times of outsourcing testing and manufacturing of their designs. It also provides a tool for makers to experiment with new types of yarns and fabrics.

CONCLUSION

THE CRAFTSMANSHIP SCENARIO IN THE NETWORKING ERA

Alessandra Rinaldi

University of Florence

The networking era and the spread of advanced digital technologies, applied to the world of design and industry 4.0, are changing the entire process of creation as well as the development of manufacturing products, starting from the generation of concepts up to design and production systems.

Because of the digital transformation and its related impact on the manufacturing Industry 4.0, the design focus - until now concerning figurative, communicative and expressive as well as technical and productive aspects of manufacturing - is moving towards perceptual, interactive and valuable issues, reaching up experience design, which becomes less physical and tactile, but more and more sensorial and virtual.

The ongoing transformation significantly impacts design and the role of designers by bringing out new paradigms for the project development of innovative products. As shown in Andrea Salvadori's research as well as in Studio Joachim-Morineau and Unfold & Tim Knapen, new tools and technologies have entered the panorama of design and production. They are impacting both the creative processes and the ways of interaction between not only designers and projects, but also designers and products. This is just the beginning of this experimentation.

The transition from standard design and production digital systems (able to help designers to find support for creative activity and design) to parametric software (which allows the production of mathematical models that could be modified as organisms), has opened up new opportunities to explore the variety of formal possibilities, allowing adaptive and interactive management. We have seen that in Kourosh Asgar-Irani's work.

Parametric and generative software as well as additive production systems are opening new horizons to the creativity of designers, offering the chance of creating both complex shapes, not achievable with other geometries, and already assembled components.

The possibilities generated by the new design tools are often associated with new production processes, no longer mechanical, but plastic, linked to the additive methods of digital fabrication (3D printing).

Thanks to fast production, also called rapid prototyping or 3D printing, design can enter the realm of the sculptural imagination while maintaining its functional and economic characteristics.

Finally, augmented reality and virtual reality are changing the ways of testing and controlling the final product, and opening up new opportunities and future innovation scenarios also for sale and distribution.

Designers shall seize the opportunities lying within these systems, by integrating and managing a complex series of variables in the design process not only from a geometric point of view, but also from a conceptual and productive one.

At the same time, a new concept of luxury arises: it is linked to values such as beauty, innovativeness and above all uniqueness, which no longer belong just to artistic and artisanal production, but become part of mass production. The products personalized directly by the end-user, the creation of projects in open design and the development of delocalized production will realistically cross the border of self-production in the near future, moving towards a large-scale production of products ready for wider markets, as we can see in Common Works and "Kniterate" trials.

Precious and unique products are made by expert artisan designers who use digital technologies to recreate the aesthetics of imperfection, the irregularity and the uniqueness of natural things. This is the case of Eric Klarenbeek and Maartje Dros' trials together with Tomaš Libertíny's ones, which recall the research conducted by some design laboratories, such as the MIT Media Lab in Boston directed by Neri Oxman. The idea is to go beyond the imitation of a biological structure in order to emphasize the implementation of a natural building process, suggesting that nature is the ultimate form-giver.

Perfection does not belong to human beings who constantly experience imperfection throughout their existence. Thus, the beauty of imperfection finds large space in this third millennium: in fashion, design, architecture and art.

In 2003 Gaetano Pesce, a famous Italian designer, presented in Milan "Nobody's perfect": a collection of ninety-nine unique pieces in resin wherein he attributes the imperfection and uniqueness of the objects to a new aesthetic value.

What emerges from the works of the designers in this book is the need to reflect on the skills and the opportunities for the next generation of designers, artists and artisans. New transversal paths will incorporate innovative sectors such as generative programming, virtual reality and augmented reality, along with experience-driven design. All these opportunities will be useful for designers to translate even the most complex visions into tangible signs.